IGNAZ MAYBAUM

CREATION AND GUILT

A Theological Assessment
of Freud's
Father-Son Conflict

Vallentine, Mitchell – London

First published in Great Britain 1969
by Vallentine, Mitchell & Co. Ltd.
18 Cursitor Street, London E.C.4

SBN 85303029 4

Printed and bound in Great Britain by
Tonbridge Printers Ltd
Peach Hall Works, Tonbridge, Kent

To

Michael and Elisabeth
Eric and Alisa
Dow and Fredzia

ACKNOWLEDGEMENTS

I am deeply indebted to my pupil Mr Nicholas de Lange of Christ Church, Oxford, who read the whole typescript of this book and not merely helped me in technical matters but has also given me important advice. As always in my writings my wife has been involved in the publication of this book. I doubt whether it would ever have come out without her help as housewife, secretary and partner, identifying herself with my work and assisting me with constructive criticism.

I also want to express my appreciation to the Rev. Hubert Hoskins, Talks Producer, Religious Broadcasting Department of the B.B.C., for the helpful suggestions he made in connection with the chapter *The Medieval Passion Play* in Part One, which was broadcast on the Third Programme of the B.B.C.

A part of the last chapter of this book, *Islamic Submission to the Law,* has been published in a collection of essays (*Studies in Rationalism, Judaism and Universalism*) commemorating the great scholar whom I mention here again with gratitude, the late Professor Leon Roth of Jerusalem University. I thank the publishers (Routledge and Kegan Paul) for permission to make use of my contribution to this volume published by them.

I am grateful to the R.S.G.B. (Reform Synagogues of Great Britain) for their assistance in my theological work.

Edgware, 1969.

CONTENTS

Then Abram . . .
. . . stretchèd forth the knife to slay his son.
When lo! an angel called him out of heaven,
Saying, Lay not thy hand upon the lad,
Neither do anything to him . . .

But the old man would not so, but slew his son,
And half the seed of Europe, one by one.

From Wilfred Owen's poem
THE PARABLE OF THE OLD MAN AND THE YOUNG
part of Benjamin Britten's WAR REQUIEM

INTRODUCTION

In 1916, six months after I had left school, I marched with a Hungarian regiment to a railway station from which cattle trucks took us to the Russian front. It was harvest time and the cornfields were a sea of gold. The harvesters were women and old men; the young were away at the war. Some of the women, interrupting their work at the sight of the marching column, knelt down and crossed themselves.

One of my comrades said: 'As if Christ were marching with us!' Another replied: 'Anyway, we shall be crucified.'

After the war I followed the tradition of my family and became a rabbi. I served congregations in Germany and England. I wrote theological books. In writing in this book that the 'Tomb of the Unknown Warrior' is the modern form of the Cross I feel I am faithful to the comrades with whom I marched under the heavy pack of the frontline-soldier.

My reader will find me concerned with a Christian theology which speaks of deicide. Freud observes a patricide. In World Wars I and II the flower of Europe's and America's youth went to the Golgotha of their battlefields. Who sent them? Did the old send the young, or did the young in the vigour of their youth force the hand of the old so that war became inevitable? What is the man on the Cross, a father or a son? I had to argue not only with the Christian theologian but also with Freud. In Judaism I find a belief in the God of the fathers, in Christianity – in so far as it is cut off from Judaism – rather a belief in the God of the sons. I had, of course, also to deal with deicide as an antisemitic slogan expressing the verbal monstrosity: 'The Jews killed Christ.'

The biblical Book of Lamentations makes most apposite

11

reading to the world in which we have lived since 1914. To this book some prophet or rabbi wrote a short postscript expressed in the verse: 'Renew our days as of old.' A romantic would understand this verse as voicing the hope that a past chapter of history should return. From this romanticism the writer of the postscript is radically aloof. He prays for man's return to the realm which is not man-made history but the eternal beginning, from which history starts. This realm, the world as God created it, not the superstructure of civilisation created by state, organised religion and culture, is populated by men, women and children, whose lives we follow when we read the Book of Genesis. We speak here of the world of the patriarchs or, to avoid this archaic word, of the fathers. The Jewish prayer asks that the blessing with which 'God blessed our fathers Abraham, Isaac and Jacob' should reach us, who stand not in the beginning from which history starts, but in the midst of history. To the world of the fathers the Christian doctrine of original sin is not applicable. Where the family is not yet destroyed by war efforts and by an all-embracing techno-logical enterprise, we still possess this world as created by God. The family lives outside history, and this life need not be primitive, as the Book of Genesis proves. The life de-scribed in this biblical book as the life of the fathers is not bourgeois life, as it seemed to Kierkegaard. True, the fathers and the bourgeois class both pursue peace and cherish stability. But no man who speaks to God 'mouth to mouth' (Numbers xii, 8) is a bourgeois. The fathers do this as family-men, as later the prophets do from outside family-life on the stage of history.

Nor is there any need in the family for the conflict be-tween father and son which Freud made the subject of his clinical observations. I have made extensive use of Freud's work. I am not concerned with Freud the doctor, the healer of mental illness. I refer to the statement he makes about historical and metaphysical subjects. I do so most critically. It will be a surprise to my reader that in my analysis of the father-son conflict I had no need to deal with the Oedipus-myth. Instead, Genesis 22, the story of Abraham and Isaac walking to the altar of sacrifice, became the centre of my book. This story with its different Jewish, Christian and Mohammedan interpretations guided me towards an understanding of the difference between and the identity of the three monotheistic religions.

I had to give ample space to Islam in my book. Our civilisation is not merely a Judaeo-Christian civilisation. There is also a considerable Islamic contribution visible to every one in the Middle Ages but today forgotten. The lack of acknowledgement of the Islamic contribution has its reason. Islamic elements were regarded as Jewish. The opposition of faith and law, love and justice separates Christianity and Islam. The Jew, because he is not shaped by the historical process, but is the direct product of the Creation, represents the human situation: man can in his existence unite faith and law, love and justice.

The Jew and the humanist are different persons. For Muslim and humanist there is no such thing as a profane world. 'The whole of this earth is a mosque,' says Mohammed. The distinction (*havdalah*) between holy and profane, on the other hand, constitutes Jewish life. The Jew has also been called the bourgeois par excellence. In this the Jew is again identified with the Muslim. The Koran stipulates: 'There is no change in God's Creation'. A bourgeois with his love of stability, may agree with this verse of the Koran. The Jew cannot. He is told by his prayer book that 'God renews the world every evening and every morning'. Praying this text the Jew confesses a belief in progress. His concept of progress co-operates with the creators of history but as a messianic belief in progress it has as its goal a return to the beginning, to the world of the fathers.

By showing the Islamic roots of the bourgeois and the humanist, my aim was not to denigrate these two mighty contributors to our civilisation but bring them back to their place in a monotheistic faith, from where they originate. The humanist, like the whole of Islam, is still connected to his Jewish-Christian origin. He is a Christian heretic. To Dante Islam was a 'Christian heresy'. This 'heresy' shaped the Middle Ages to a higher degree than the Christian Church. 'Heresies there must be', says Paul (I Cor. xi, 19). I understand this word of Paul to mean that history moves dialectically, one thesis creating its antithesis. 'Legalistic' Judaism is a slogan of Pauline Christianity, Judaism requires no spiritual counterbalance. Judaism is human life as the fathers lived it; Judaism is the 'holy seed', as the Jewish people is called in a parable quoted in this book. The 'holy seed' of Judaism gives birth to Christianity and Islam. I do not see the bourgeois as guilty of stagnation, but I see him in his possible relationship to the 'fathers' of the Book of Genesis, who are the guardians of the eternal order. By stressing that the roots of the humanist and the bourgeois lie in their Islamic and Christian origin, I hope to convince them that a belief in God has once made them what they are. Only this belief can prevent the humanist from lapsing into barbarism and the bourgeois from lapsing into decadence.

Besides the humanist and the bourgeois stands the citizen-soldier, acting out the human *comedia divina,* the tragedy of our age. The symbol of the Cross takes on a hallowed meaning in view of the many millions of soldiers, sailors and airmen who died that their kith and kin could live and enjoy the good life of the children of God. Sacrificial love and vicarious suffering make the citizen-soldier of the Christian world a hero adorned with the halo of the martyr. In our nuclear age war, global war, would be suicide. It would be the end of that sacrificial love and vicarious suffering which soldiers have displayed in the two thousand years of Christianity which were two thousand years of wars. In an atomic war nobody would die for anybody else, but all would die together. Nobody would benefit by the sacrifice of an individual, but all would become sufferers and would be destroyed. On the Golgotha of atomic war no Cross can be

erected. Golgotha would become what the Hebrew word
originally meant: a 'place of skulls'. The Golgotha of atomic
war would become what Auschwitz was, not a place of
heroism but a place of the martyrdom of de-humanised mankind. I speak of the *churban** of Auschwitz: *Churban* means
'destruction'. The *churban* of Auschwitz is dealt with in this
book not merely because its author is a Jew. There was the
wider theological necessity to see the *churban* of Auschwitz
in the light of 'The Apocalypse of John', showing that a
historical situation can arise where the Cross with its message
of love has no application. In an atomic war the lot of mankind would be no longer history but an apocalyptic catastrophe. No 'Tomb of the Unknown Warrior' could possibly
be erected after an atomic war. The 'unknown warrior' would
be well known. He would be mankind. *Pax* proclaims the
message 'Love your enemies'; *shalom* demands a world without enemies. Our world cries out for *shalom,* for the peace in
which man is not a warrior, in which he lives in his family,
eats his bread, fully employs his faculties and dies contented
at a ripe old age. History consumes its hecatombs of human
sacrifice. Our world cries out for the world of the fathers
as the Book of Genesis describes it.

The manuscript of this book was finished when the Six-
Day War between the Israelis and the Arabs made head-
lines all over the world. But it would be a grave omission
if my introduction did not refer to the new situation created
by the Six-Day War. I have written this book as a Jew who
believes in the possibility of Jewish existence under the conditions of the Diaspora. I do not agree with the view which
assumes that a community lacking power is a despicable
pariah-community. Who, after all, has power in the world of
the giants? Jews bidden to show mankind the example of
living in dignity without wielding power have been forced to
make Israel a military fortress. In the Six-Day War the Jews
proved themselves good soldiers. This they had learnt from
the gentiles.

* The 'ch' is pronounced as in the Scottish word loch.

15

Greek antiquity had the concept of the tragic hero, seen as standing on the highest level of human existence. Where Greece praises the battling demigod, the Jew praises the servant of God. The Jew is bidden by God to be a priest, and the priest wanders through the world without wielding a sword. Christianity changed the nature of the Greek hero and pointed to sacrificial love, in which the hero dies for others. Christianity sees one hero, shedding his blood for his fellow man, in a status entirely equal to God. From that moment in history the soldier, ready to die for others, harbours holy sacrificial love in his own heart. The Israeli soldiers died in this way. They are therefore part of this noble and spiritual Christian history! The Servant of God, bidden in the Isaiah-texts to be a priest, became in modern Israel a soldier. All glory to him! I profess this glory as a Jew who fully understands the Christian virtue of sacrificial love. Battle and glory – we Jews did not ponder about them, after the Book of Daniel was written. In this book the question is asked: What about those who die fighting to save their kith and kin? The answer in this case became the hope and consolation of all men: we do not die into the grave, we die into the eternity of God. As martyrs we Jews died as courageously as do heroes. We were able to be an unarmed nation for two thousand years.

The Jew praises the unconditional love of God in the story which tells that Isaac was not sacrificed. The Christian too praises the unconditional love of God but changes the story. A sacrificed Isaac on the Cross heralds the love of one who laid down his life for others. Jewish fathers in Israel, mourning the death in battle of their sons, will find that consolation which Christians find looking to the man on the Cross: he died for us. A Jew forced to think in this way is no longer Abraham. Franz Rosenzweig expressed the view that a Jewish State might bring Jews near to Christian doctrine. Christian faith always rises out of Jewish soil. This is the glory of the Jews. But Jews desire to remain Jews.

The Jew represents nothing else than the human situa-

16

tion. It is human that fathers would not sacrifice their sons for any prospect which a particular situation may offer. It is different in the situation of heroic man, creative in politics and history, the superstructure which spans men's private lives. Political history consumes men. Sacrifice is the price which must be paid. Had Abraham lost his son in the trial in which his faith was tested, he would have lost everything. Having only the universal mission to be a blessing for mankind, Abraham cannot fulfil his mission, unless he is a father. The son inherits the mission of the father. The king of Moab who sacrifices his son (II Kings iii, 27) does not lose everything. He loses his son, but instead he gains victory in battle.

Stalin's son Yakov was captured by the Germans in the year 1941. Stalin refused an exchange which was offered. He said to his daughter Svetlana: 'War is war.' Yakov perished. Harold Nicholson, not a monster like Stalin, but a noble Christian Englishman, declared that 'he would rather have it that his son were killed at Cassino than that the monastery should be destroyed'. 'Works of art', he argues, 'are irreplaceable, whereas no lives are irreplaceable.'

Stalin and Nicholson do not hear the voice of the angel calling to Abraham 'Lay not thy hand upon the lad, neither do thou anything unto him.' Stalin and Nicholson know of a situation in which they feel bound to act heroically and to sacrifice their own flesh and blood. Gentile history is full of heroism, a super-human heroism indeed, in which fathers approve of the sacrifice of their sons for political and cultural causes. But the eyes of the Jew see what is inhuman in the super-human enterprise. Is the Jewish people in Israel, crowned with the laurels of the Six-Day War, still the Jewish people, saluting all mankind with the word *shalom*? There is good reason to answer this important question in the affirmative. The Israeli soldier fought to save the lives of women and children. Had the Israelis lost, the Arabs would have done what the Germans did: genocide would have taken place on the soil of the holy land. The battle of the Warsaw Ghetto which the Jews lost in Poland, was won in Israel. The

Jews fighting the Six-Day War had no secular objective. The Israeli soldier was not infatuated with the glory of heroism. He fought to save Jewish homes. The Israeli soldier is a citizen-soldier, a Jew for whom fighting and killing is never a profession which can be surrounded with a halo. Men at war re-enact Cain's killing of Abel. The Jew is a man who regards peace as the holiest aim of mankind. This is not pacifism. Situations can arise where pacifism is suicide. In the war against Hitler pacifism in the western camp was immoral. The fight of the Israeli citizen-soldier has the same dignity of moral justification and the same moral necessity as the war against Hitler.

Persecuted and oppressed people look with eschatological hope towards a future of freedom and security. The persecuted and oppressed Jews were led to Zion by their eschatological hope. Eschatology is blind to reality. The reality was a country populated by Arabs. The Zionists saw Palestine as an empty country which might without objection become a Jewish home. She was neglected by oriental stagnation and had in many places become desert. In the true innocence which the Liberals often displayed towards history, Theodor Herzl said of Palestine: 'A country without a people, for the people without a country'. Jews were soon taught the hard lesson that the country belonged to the Arabs. Two rights clashed, the right of the Arabs, and the right of the Jews. The Christian emphasises that history always harbours a guilt within itself. Guilt can be atoned through love. The Jews lavished their love on their disputed homeland. With the sweat of their brow and with sacrifices of many sorts they made the desert bloom and called it the Jewish home. The pilgrim prayed: 'Blessed be the Lord, that has given rest to His people Israel according to all that He promised' (I Kings, viii, 56). Yet there was no rest. The eschatological vision of final peace faded and history proceeded with all its predicaments. The Jew had to fight. He was forced into this situation contrary to his mission.

Books about the Jewish contribution to the civilisation

18

of Europe and America abound. Encyclopaedic volumes record what the diaspora Jews did for their various homelands. To Abraham it is said: 'I will bless them that bless thee' (Genesis xii, 3). Where Jews have peace, the gentiles participate in this gift of God. Peace is indivisible. Where Jews are persecuted, the whole country is doomed. Everybody will soon be denied what the Jew is denied. It begins with the suppression of the Jews; what follows is that the gentiles themselves are deprived of freedom, prosperity, security; in short, everybody will be denied the blessings of peace. '...and him that curses thee will I curse' (Genesis, ibid.). From Abraham to this present hour and for all future time the mission of the Jewish people is not to convert others but every individual Jew has the mission expressed in the words said to Abraham: '...in thee shall all the families of the earth be blessed' (Genesis, ibid.). The Jewish mission aims at the wellbeing of all mankind.

Before and after the first world war a fierce controversy raged among Jews about the doctrine of a Jewish mission. It was the time when circumstances in Eastern Europe made Jewish life appear more and more untenable. Immigration to America had nearly stopped and the Zionist solution was the only proposal for an exit to freedom. Zionists brushed aside the idea of a Jewish mission with an only too logical argument: When your own people is in need of being rescued from deadly danger, do not think of a universal commitment to mankind. Save your people! Zionists were angry when their opponents quoted Isaiah xlix, 6 '...It is too light a thing that thou shouldest be My servant To raise up the tribes of Jacob, And to restore the offspring of Israel; I will also give thee for a light to the nations, That My salvation may be unto the end of the earth.' That is for better times, said the Zionists. The persecuted, hungry, despised need help. Let us go to Zion. Some went. Six million perished under Hitler. Were the Zionists not right? Were the Non-Zionists not wrong? The controversy between these two groups is to be found within the

Book of Isaiah itself. It gives the Jewish Diaspora a mission to mankind and teaches the ingathering of the exiles as messianic hope. For believers the messianic fulfilment is 'round the corner'.

The universal mission to serve mankind – to be a light unto the gentiles, as Isaiah puts it – does not allow the Jews to feel superior to the gentiles. History is gentile history, and it remains the stage from which the Jewish people must not withdraw for the sake of its service of mankind. This service can only be done in the humility of the worker whose work is done away from the limelight. The public hears of the Jewish Nobel-prize winners but does not hear of the thousands of Jews who expedite the welfare of the country of their exile. Blessing is a decisive force. Blessing spreads happiness. But blessing cannot be catalogued, not even in those many volumes which register in encyclopaedic form the contribution of Jewry to human civilisation.

In Israel itself the wish to get out of the iron ring of isolation and to be accepted by the family of nations has led to the rendering of technological assistance to African and Asian countries by devoted individuals and by institutions. The wish to be 'a light to the nations', the wish to revive Isaiah's concept of a Jewish mission now wakes in the Zionist camp itself. The next step would be to apply the Jewish mission to the Arabs. The Jew does not want to be the enemy of the Arab; he desires to be a blessing to him. The Arabs are now waking from their Middle Ages and want to move into the new era of western civilisation. Obviously the Jew can be of help to the Arab in his leap forward.

The Jew has become a blessing to the whole of western civilisation. This is on record, as every student of history will testify. The carrier of blessing is able to fulfil his mission when love motivates him. The Jews have always fallen in love with the people in whose midst they lived. How the German Jews loved Germany! How Eastern European Jews loved their countries in spite of persecution! How we loved Spain! Out of the great love of Jews for Greece sprung two new world civilisations: Christianity and Islam. The Jews, given the political opportunity of peaceful neighbourhood will love the Arabs, too. To the eyes of those who know Jewish history, this prediction does not appear strange. The Arabs were once a great nation with a civilisation which was in the Middle Ages superior to that of Europe. As German Jews quoted the German classics with relish, Jews, having studied Arabic literature at Jerusalem university, can become acquainted with Arabic culture. Hand in hand with an Arab-Jewish communion by books goes the bond of trade which unites the Jewish with the Arab businessman. Arab-Jewish fellowship – is this a dream? Theodor Herzl concluded his book *The Jewish State* with the words: 'If you wish it – it is no fairy tale.' Arab-Jewish fellowship – if you wish it – is no fairy tale.

The State of Israel will not bring about the end of the Jewish diaspora. The Israeli politicians hope to attract many western Jews, but none of them envisages an end of the diaspora. What has been achieved by Israel is that the Jewish people has been moved back to the stage of history. Gentiles and Christians can no longer see the Jews as isolated individuals, but must see them as a people. They must ask: What is the role of this people within mankind? The Holy Scriptures of the Jews provide the answer to this question.

Part One

DEICIDE

THE MEDIEVAL PASSION PLAY

The medieval passion play is performed in Oberammergau and other centres on the Continent. Recently it could be seen in England. If we were to give a title to the tragedy represented and enacted here, it would be, surely 'deicide' – 'the killing of God'. The notion of 'deicide' has traditionally been associated in Christendom with the Jewish people, with the idea that in the crucifixion the Jews were responsible for 'the death of God'. Deicide, then, has been much under discussion, especially during and since the second Vatican Council held by the Roman Catholic Church. Accusations levelled at the Jews have been softened, or modified, or even retracted. But the issues at stake, from a Jewish as well as a Christian standpoint, have still not been thoroughly clarified.

The formulation 'the Jews killed Christ' does not dominate the New Testament. It is not a dogma. Yet it is a doctrine for which the established Church is fully responsible. The Church is responsible for the fact that the Jews were branded with the stigma of deicide. Yet inseparable from the New Testament are Paul's words about the Jews in Romans XI: 'God has not rejected the people which He acknowledged of old as his own'.

Christian theology is now in duty bound to emancipate the concept of deicide from a pre-Christian myth, and from serving as an antisemitic doctrine. That is why those of us who are committed to the Jewish-Christian dialogue must include the passion play in the agenda of our discussions.

How does the medieval passion play in fact envisage the event of the crucifixion? The question 'Who killed Christ?' makes anyone who watches the play look automatically to Pilate and his soldiers. They represent imperial

25

Rome which wields power over the life and death of all. But the Jews were the unfree subjects of this power. They obeyed, either with the resentment of the opponent or with the bad conscience of the collaborator. To those who staged the passion play in the Middle Ages, the role of the Romans was clear. They were the central figures.

The passion play shows Christ on his way to the crucifixion accompanied by the Roman soldiers. Christ carries the cross, the instrument which the Romans used for capital punishment. The Roman soldiers carry their weapons. The crown of thorns on the head of Christ is a torture invented by the brutal soldiers. The onlooker sees all this: Christ in the hands of cruel heathens. The onlooker of the passion play also sees the Jews walking with the soldiers. But the Jews are merely there in order to offer themselves to the gaze of the crowd. They are merely 'extras'. They are, of course, ridiculed as fat and bearded bourgeois. The fattest and most bourgeois-looking of the Jews is staged as High Priest.

The action of the play, in spite of its crudeness, is in harmony with the truth that the Romans, not the Jews, are charged with cruelty towards Christ. The play ends, of course, with the cry: 'Crucify him, crucify him!' But even here the visual side is correct in its portrayal of history. The shouting is addressed to Pilate who alone has the power to crucify anyone, so that the lesson of the play 'The Jews killed Christ' is not borne out by what the onlooking mob really sees. As long as the play remains in its visual frame, it gives the real content of the Gospel story which states – as scientific historical exegesis now emphasises – that the Jewish court, the sanhedrin, had no power of capital jurisdiction. Jesus of Nazareth was crucified. This was done by the Romans, who alone had the power to do it. Christ and the Jews were both the sufferers. The man executed by the Romans on the cross and the Jews were one in the misery which a triumphant Rome heaped on their shoulders.

Recently, on television, the passion play as performed

in Franco's Spain, was shown. It was grand theatre. The armour and the weapons of the Roman soldiers were authentic and the costumed Jews were just as medieval men imagined them. It was a first class production. Hollywood could not have done better. Franco was on view, too, in a large saloon car; and Christ was there with his crown of thorns, bent under the burden of the heavy cross. The visual effect of the play was inevitably that of a triumphal procession. The man who triumphed was Franco.

The man bearing his cross represented all those whom the triumphant man had sent to their death, all those who languished in the Spanish prisons, all those who had to leave Spain and become homeless. Any passion play is a triumphal procession; and the watching audience must recognise who plays which role. In Auschwitz Hitler was the triumphant Caesar; and at Golgotha it was the Roman Eagle that triumphed.

What a display of barbaric pomp in the triumphal procession of the Roman Caesar! His face is painted red with minium like the statue of Jupiter on the Capitol. In his hand is the eagle sceptre. Over his head are held the insignia of glory, the triumphal wreath of gold and diamonds. His quadriga is drawn by snow-white horses, and around it the soldiers prance in three-step as the worshippers of the Caesar-God.

Triumph in origin means 'three-step'. In the triumphal procession they do not walk the ordinary way, they walk one step and then stamp with both feet in the orgy of their victory. Hitler danced his jig in front of the film cameras after the fall of France, and Franco rode in his saloon car in the passion play to celebrate the anniversary of his victory in the Civil War. The Roman triumphal procession had its many horrors. The prisoners were tortured, female prisoners had to lift up their skirts while walking in the procession, everything indecent was permitted to the soldiers with impunity. Victory meant that the Caesar was God, creating his own law.

If the passion play makes the Jews a defeated and guilty group – as the medieval play does – then it becomes a pagan, triumphal procession. It makes the Cross a sign of victory over the Jews. The Cross ceases to tell of the God of Abraham, Isaac and Jacob in the clash with Rome, but tells of the victory of Rome over the Jews, as Titus' Arch glorifies it. *Judaea capta,* behold, Judaea is defeated! – an event celebrated no longer by Roman heathens, but staged in Oberammergau, in Tegelen in Holland, in Mexico and in South America.

It is important to establish what the Christian doctrine enshrined in the passion play has in common, first, with the theme of the 'suffering servant' in the 'Servant of God' texts of the Old Testament and then with the Promethean myth of the Greeks – important too, however, to distinguish the differences between them. Christian exegesis which searches for Christian teaching within the Old Testament has, traditionally at any rate, pointed to the 'Servant of God' texts in the Book of Isaiah. The Servant of God, this prophet whose name we do not know, is brought to his doom by a power outside the Jewish people, probably by the last Babylonian king. So far it is exactly like the narrative of the Gospels. But there is a striking difference. The Babylonian holder of power does not enter the stage on which we see the suffering prophet. There is no stage. There is no Babylonian Pilate in the 'Servant of God' texts, nor is there a Herod. According to the Synoptic Gospels on the other hand, Pilate and the Roman soldiers are manifestly involved in the crucifixion of Christ. No parallel exists in the 'Servant of God' texts to the variety of roles and scenarios in the New Testament.

The 'Servant of God' texts on the one hand, and the synoptic Gospels recording the Passion of Christ on the other, are, as literary types, as different from each other as for example a prose epic from a tragic play. The authors of the Gospels followed the Greek prototype of classical tragedy and dramatised into a clash between individual and authority what is in the Hebrew text the story of a Jew, the story of a

28

man chosen by God and, in the words of Isaiah, 'despised and forsaken by man'. The Gospels bring on the stage Jews and Romans, Christ and the High Priest, the disciples and Pilate. When the authors of the Gospels make the Jews shout 'crucify him, crucify him!' it is clear that the Jews have been given the role of the chorus of Greek tragedy. The chorus makes articulate the will of one individual or of several individuals which decides the way in which the tragedy inevitably develops. The chorus is the voice of fate. Has the High Priest or Pilate, have the Jews or the Romans, become articulate in the voice of the chorus shouting 'crucify him, crucify him!'? The tragic playwright does not give an answer to such a question. He lets his audience watch the play. They have eyes to see and can judge for themselves. The medieval passion play starts in the Gospels.

In the Greek story of Prometheus we find points of both identity with, and difference from, the Gospels' narratives of the 'deicide'. According to Greek mythology, Prometheus, who represents creative man, is chained to a rock. Vultures eat the liver from his living body. The rebel who wants to be what God is, a creator, is punished for his *Hubris,* for his sin of attempting to be God-like. The story expresses the deep pessimism of the Greek who, above all, wanted to be a poi-ètès, a maker of things, whether these things were marble wonders of sculpture, works of literature, states or empires. In this, his deepest desire, he was stricken with the knowledge of the futility of his desire. He knew he would not reach final success. The absolute solution would evade him.

Five hundred years after the myth of Prometheus was expressed as the philosophy of pessimism, a Cross was erected on Golgotha. It became a symbol which brought hope to the languishing Hellenistic world of the Mediterranean basin. In the symbol of the Cross the old symbol, that of Prometheus on the rock, was still recognisable. But the new symbol changed the gentile world. The philosophy of despair was silenced. The Cross had its message of good tidings for man who suffered in his Promethean enterprise as artist, politician, planner, in short, as a poi-ètès, maker of things. The message was: Death on the Cross is not an end. It is a beginning. It is the death of a son, who ceases to be a son and becomes in his own right what the father is – creator.

The man on the Cross is not what Prometheus is: a rebel. On the Cross he is at one with the father.

Christians and Jews, both, must surely object to the one-sided way in which Freud deals with deicide as the outcome of the father-son conflict in the subconscious mind. Freud only sees a cruel father and a rebellious son. In Auschwitz rebellious sons have killed fathers. Freud saw it coming. But his depth-psychology, developed in antisemitic Vienna, did not enable him to see the sacrificial love of the sons uniting them with the fathers. Yet, the sacrifice of the sons in their attempt to improve the world of the fathers is enormous, enormous is the sacrifice of the sons on the battlefields of history.

In view of what has been said, it is from the Christian premises themselves a travesty of the Gospels to ask 'Who killed Christ?', as if his death could have been avoided like a mishap or a judicial murder. From the point of view of the synoptic Gospels, the deicide could not have been avoided in this way. The Gospels used the image of deicide to contradict the Greek tragic playwrights, who speak of fate inevitably leading man to his doom. In the deicide the Gospels describe a tragedy, but one which in a most un-Greek manner leads to a happy ending. The peace-lacking gentile at last receives the message of peace.

Those who have killed Jews from the time of Constantine's union of Church and State up to Auschwitz are themselves involved in the sacrilege of deicide. They have shouted their antisemitic 'crucify him! crucify him!' and with this same cry demanded the death of the Jews. The antisemitic 'crucify him, crucify him!' became the Nazi slogan 'Perish Judah!' The first crusade was also a pogrom.

The present discussion about deicide will not change

Christian faith, and is not intended to do so. Jewish semantics have the figure of a king and father or of a prophet, who, as Messiah, leads towards the goal of history. The Jewish people faithfully waits for what is not yet but what will come: the kingdom of justice, mercy and truth. Jews as Jews 'walk without a sideward glance through history', said Franz Rosenzweig.

The Christian cries out in jubilation: The tragedies of history receive their happy ending, the Cross contradicts tragedy, the sacrifices on the battlefields of history are not meaningless. All those who stand astride in the path of history have in the crucified and resurrected God-man the guarantee of victory and bliss. History is not 'a story told by an idiot', it is Golgotha and Calvary, crucifixion and resurrection. The deicide in which the servants of God suffer and die makes history progress ever nearer towards redemption.

The Jewish jubilation about the God-created world sees the world of the fathers as the blissful habitation of man; as for history – the miracle at the Red Sea guarantees God's victory outside the world of the fathers. In the world of the fathers men are born, grow up, woo, marry and beget children and live under eternal laws in the happiness of the creatures of God.

The study of the difference between Judaism and Christianity is the heart and soul of any Jewish-Christian dialogue worthy of the name. In regard to the concept of deicide the difference between Jew and Christian is clear, and this difference must not be blurred. A Jewish theology, faithful to the content of the Hebrew Bible, can see no reference to deicide either in the 'Servant of God' texts of the Book of Isaiah or in Genesis 22 which tells mankind that Isaac was not sacrificed and which proclaims the message of love uniting father and son. Jew and Christian are both witnesses of God. Jewish is the rejoicing that Isaac is not sacrificed. Christianity is the triumphant faith that a sacrificed Isaac bestows the glory of redemption on mankind.

THE CRUSADERS

When the combat is over, a battlefield renders not only a sad picture but also a scene of ghastly horror. What has happened? Man, the creature of God, 'not lower than the angels' has been sacrilegiously assaulted. There lie the slain, their mouths gaping, their wounds open, one or more limbs missing – the image of God, the Creator, dragged into a mud of blood and earth. Death inflicted on man by man is sacrilege against God, the Creator of man. The post-war generation has now seen on the television screen what happened to the youth of two world wars. Our generation has awakened to a compassionate interest in the suffering and dying of soldiers, sailors and airmen, and wonders what reaction would be honest and truly human. There is the word deicide. Let those who mourn the dead whom we remember on Remembrance Day cry out: deicide. The child of God has been sacrificed and killed. God in man was attacked on the battlefield, and deicide was the sin committed by man.

The picture of a battlefield after the battle is over says to the surviving generation 'It is accomplished' (John xix, 30). This 'It is accomplished' means the job which had to be done is now done – for the benefit of the surviving generation. The Cross is also a sad and horrible picture. To say this, is not irreverence, but is in true harmony with the Christian creed. The last word of the man on the Cross was, we are told, 'It is accomplished'. This means: My suffering and dying were unavoidable; they were necessary for the redemption of pagan history. Yet the Christian, hailing God the Redeemer, is asked by the Jew: what about God the Creator? Is not the God of Abraham, Isaac and Jacob also

32

the victorious God of the Red Sea, is He not both Creator and Redeemer?

Do the rise of a Jewish State and the world-wide proclamation of a Jewish-Christian fellowship initiate a new chapter in the pilgrimage of the Jewish people through the world? A new chapter in the eternal, unchanging Jewish life may now begin. What is eternal, can always become new. What is not possible, is the transformation of the Jewish people into a 'new Israel'. It is a mistake to concentrate all attention on what is called the 'miraculous' rise of a Jewish State and see the world-Diaspora of modern Jewry without that light which shines for all mankind. The miracles which sanctify the history of the Jewish people have occurred in the Diaspora. The State of Israel is itself a part of the Jewish Diaspora and is not outside it.

The Crusaders were described by Gibbon under the heading 'The World's Debate'. The debate about the crusades has not yet stopped. Were the Crusaders saints in armour? Or were they cruel heathens who as baptised heathens could regard themselves as chosen to wage God's war? Trevor-Roper writes:

> 'At first, the view was clear enough. The simple crusaders, who paused to chronicle their violent but holy deeds, and ended each chapter of carnage with devout scriptural ejaculations, questioned their own motives no more than the Spanish conquistadores of the sixteenth century; and even five or six centuries later their learned historians calmly echoed their sentiments. At the court of Louis XIV the fashionable Jesuit Louis Maimbourg gloried in the massacre of the infidels, how the Christians "killed the very children . . . to exterminate if possible, that accursed race, as God formerly wished to be done to the Amalekites".'
>
> *(The Rise of Christian Europe, p. 101.)*

The Jesuit preacher quotes Deut. xxv, 17, where what is commanded is not the extermination of the Amalekites but 'the blotting out of the *remembrance* of Amalek'. A rabbinical commentary points to the parallel text of Exodus xvii, 14 where the 'blotting out' is done by God and not by the children of Israel. The Book of Joshua is even more problematical for the Jew, called 'merciful and son of merciful ones'. Proper reading of this book teaches that God is always the last victor of all battles, always the Law-giver who, if obeyed, gives blessing, and if disobeyed, punishes. Although the Book of Joshua records conquests and battles, it eventually conveys Zechariah's message (iv, 6) 'Not by military might nor by power, but by My spirit, saith the Lord of Hosts.' The author of the Book of Joshua was a priest, who never wielded a sword, nor fought a battle, nor saw blood-shed in fighting.

Whenever man dies by the hand of man, it is appropriate to speak of deicide. Man is created in the image of God. When Cain kills Abel, he lifts his murderous hand against God. Auschwitz is the place of the deicide of our time. Six million times deicide was committed. It happened in the full light of contemporary history. The question, therefore, of who were the killers, can be answered. Those who killed the six million Jews were baptised gentiles. The Christian is a baptised gentile.

Part Two

PATRICIDE

SIGMUND FREUD'S VIENNA

Israel Zangwill wrote a short story which illuminates the father-son relationship as it existed not only in the Jewry of Victorian London but everywhere where a westernised and a not yet westernised Jewry lived in close proximity. Zangwill introduces us to a Jewish writer, accompanied by his girl friend, a gentile actress. They have just hailed a cab to drive to the theatre. At this moment an old bearded Jew in outlandish garb rushes forward and calls to the writer: 'Isaac'. The writer, who is the son of the caller, rushes the actress into the cab, jumps in himself, and tells the cabby to drive off quickly. The actress asks: 'Who is this man?' The writer answers: 'Some old beggar.'

Arthur Schnitzler's novel *Der Weg ins Freie* ('The Way to Freedom') shows the same tragic father-son conflict by referring to an event which became one of the long discussed scandals of pre-1914 Vienna. 'Yesterday at noon Oskar (the son of a rich Jewish father) passed the Church of St. Michael and raised his hat. You know that at present to be religious is considered the height of fashion in atheistic Vienna. It scarcely needs explaining: Oskar, by behaving as a Roman Catholic, wanted to make a favourable impression on the group of young aristocratic officers just leaving the Church. God knows how often he had acted like that in the past without being exposed as a cheat. Yesterday, unfortunately, old Ehrenberg (the father) happened to pass by at that very moment. He saw Oskar raising his hat in front of the church. Infuriated and unable to control himself, he charged towards his son and slapped his face. For Oskar, a cavalry officer, to be publicly assaulted in this way meant the end of his social life . . . He attempted suicide which cost him an eye but

restored his honour in the club world of high society.'
(Fischer Verlag, 1928)

In the last decades of the decaying Austro-Hungarian
Empire, Vienna, where Freud lived, had its writers, artists
and scientists who made the capital of the Hapsburg
monarchy a world famous centre, an Athens on the banks
of the Danube. Many of these men were Jews. The government was in the hands of a decadent but cultured aristocracy.
The *casa Austria,* called by the nationalists 'prison of nations'
was in fact a happy place to live in until the First World
War put an end to the precarious co-existence of the new
nationalities. When Freud (1856–1939) was thirty-four years
old and had all his creative years still before him, the
Emperor Franz Joseph (1830–1917) wrote on his sixtieth
birthday to his wife: 'Slowly one becomes *ein Trottel*' (an
imbecile old man). But there were still twenty-eight years
granted to the dying Empire on the Danube, into which
Galicia, a part of Poland with a large Jewish population, had
been incorporated on the partition of Poland after the Seven
Years' War. Bohemia and Hungary with their capitals
Prague and Budapest successfully followed the pattern of life
of the glorious Viennese metropolis. In the nineteenth century
Jews left the small Hungarian and Bohemian villages and
towns and moved to the capitals. They fled from the
economic disadvantages and the intellectual narrowness of
the provincial villages which slept in their medieval world.
During the Middle Ages Jews had their economic function
in these places. On the banks of the Danube, beginning at
the outskirts of medieval Vienna and extending down to the
estuary of the Danube on the Black Sea there were in the
centre of each village the village Church, the castle of the
local count, and the Jewish shop. The 'shop' where pots and
pans, agricultural implements and also alcoholic drinks were
sold was part of the dwelling place of a family. It was at
the same time in a way a fortress protecting the inhabitants
against often unruly or drunken peasants.

After Joseph II, the Jews had become accepted as one

of the various nationalities which inhabited the *casa Austria*. When the Austrian Germans, the Hungarians, the Czechs, the Slovaks, the Serbs and the Italians destroyed the 'House of Austria', the Jews, says A. J. P. Taylor, were the only people to stand up for the universalism which the Hapsburgs had preserved for so long. This universalism was the best the Christian Middle Ages could offer to a nationalistic age. 'In my village,' the story of a Hungarian goes, 'I quite often saw in my childhood the local rabbi and the local Catholic priest walking together and chatting with each other.' Of course, they were the only 'intellectuals' in the place and they enjoyed each other's company. They were the representatives of a civilisation which once existed in Christian Europe, though for short periods and in small circles only (see Part IV).

Metternich, hailing from the Rhineland, felt that Austria-Hungary did not belong to Europe. 'Asia,' he said, 'begins with the *Landstrasse,* the road out of Vienna to the East. Franz Josef told Theodore Roosevelt: 'You see in me the last monarch of the old school.' If the Emperor meant by that that he was conscious of belonging to the wrong century, his remark was correct. He was the last monarch whose non-constitutional authority rested on the belief in the authority of an anointed kingship. This belief originated in the Old Testament and was a decisive force in medieval Christian political life. The French historian Marc Bloch, an authority on French medieval history, warned all students of the Middle Ages that nobody could understand the Middle Ages unless he was able to relive the reality of Christian belief at the coronation service in which the kings were crowned as rulers of France.

Of this Jewish-Christian belief nothing was alive any more at the court of Franz Josef. He and Emperor Wilhelm were stop-gaps at the end of the Middle Ages. The authority of both was without the sanction of a belief. It was an authority expediently upheld in the interest of a privileged minority but not respected by the member of the new society, as the industrial age and mass nationalism had created him.

An authority without religious sanction was in Germany and Austria the malaise already before Hitler. Hitler made visible to all that authority without sanctification is cruel tyranny. A generation without trust in God inherits a society in which man does not trust man, in which man is a wolf to man.

In Vienna, the Jews who flocked to the capital after 1848 mingled with the few Jews who had been there before that time. Some of these earlier Jewish residents were as Court Jews even raised to the nobility. After 1848 the non-westernised Jews in Vienna and in the provinces became integrated into the no longer medieval surroundings. The integration was the result of the process of westernisation. The Jew in Austria-Hungary became westernised to a high degree. The German language dominated the court, the army, the civil service, and the press. In Prague, Zagreb and Budapest German was the language of public life, and the Jews spoke German well, and wrote in German. The transition from Yiddish to German was easy. Yiddish was after all based on medieval German. The transition from the old times to the modern way of life shaped the Jews everywhere. In Vienna westernised and non-westernised Jews, orthodox Jews and Jews formed by liberal humanist ideas mingled, and as it is natural in a period of transition, often did so in an atmosphere of controversy. In Freud's home too the two different worlds also existed during his childhood years, and nobody can understand Freud without understanding his Jewish background.

Freud never submitted himself to analysis by a colleague. Such an analysis would have brought to his knowledge his own relationship to his father. It was the relationship of a westernised son to a non-westernised Jewish father. This relationship can create situations such as Zangwill's short story, mentioned above, describes. A son, even a loving son, can subconsciously feel hatred towards his father.

JEWISH SELF-HATRED

There was hatred in everything Freud felt and said concerning the religion of his father, and also concerning Christianity. He could not even enjoy the paintings of the great masters, because they so often dealt with religion. He fought a battle with his relatives about his wedding which he wanted to be without the Jewish religious ceremonies. He was determined that his wife should give up her 'religious prejudices'. There is some disagreement between Freud's biographer Ernest Jones and Freud's family. Jones is inclined to regard Freud's father as an orthodox Jew, the Freud family denies this and speaks of him as a freethinker. But it is not necessary to emphasize the tension between orthodox Jew and freethinker in order to arrive at the subconscious hatred in the father-son relationship which an analysis of Freud would discover. The tension between westernised son and not yet westernised father justifies the analyst in speaking of such subconscious hatred.

Had Freud submitted himself to psycho-analysis, he might have been told that he hated his father. Subconsciously he did. He hated his father when he made *kiddush*. As a child Freud must have seen this ceremony in which the eve of Sabbath and Festival is sanctified at the family table of a Jewish home. Freud hated his father when he said Grace and perhaps mumbled it in the lax manner of a Jew who still observes the custom of saying this long prayer after the meal, but no longer observes it with the respect of the convinced adherent. Freud hated his father when he observed the Sabbath rest, and he hated him when he presided at the *Seder* table on the Passover nights. This posthumous analysis is borne out by a sociological study by Theodor Lessing which describes not Freud himself, but the whole set of Freud's Jewish circle. Lessing's book is entitled *Jewish Self-Hatred*.

The westernised Freud, struggling for emancipation from the past, hated religion. In everything connected with religion an exclusive reduction to an impersonal scientific approach is impossible. In matters of religion you either love or you hate. Where God is concerned, man cannot be neutral. Man is by nature a worshipper: he worships either God or Moloch. Freud with his hate turned to the stories of primitive tribes and found there the story of a patricide, believed to be the event causing the subsequent salvation of the tribe. According to the story of the primitive tribe the sons gained their freedom through the murder of their father. With this tale Freud undertook to explain religion. All the ethnologists call it nonsense and a fairy tale, but Freud adhered to it with stubbornness in the face of scientific contradiction. He rationalised his own hatred of his father by using – or rather misusing – material from primitive ages.

He rationalised the historical situation as it existed all over Europe. There was a fatherless generation, a generation which did not experience sonship because the old age and the new age were turned against each other in hostility. 'Fatherless generation' has become a sociological term which can be applied even where the fathers are alive. The question is, do the fathers understand their role as fathers, and can they successfully play this role? Since 1914, so many fathers have died in the wars, and owing to political and economic changes so many children have not experienced home life. We call God Father, and we call religion trust, *bitachon.* Trust, security and peace are experienced in the home. The young who grow up with the protection of father and mother have trust. A fatherless generation is without security, is therefore without trust, and is therefore agnostic or atheistic.

Our prayer book, our psalms, our *midrashim,* in fact our whole religious literature speaks of God as Father. *'Avinu, Malkeinu,* our Father, our King!' This may be called symbolic language, but it concerns the reality of God. God *is* King, God *is* Father. God is King – obey him! God is Father – trust him! It is in his obedience to and his trust in his father in heaven that the Jew is a Jew. The Jew, as a father obeyed and trusted by a son, by his children, has a priestly role. In England a priest is called 'Father', in France 'mon père', in other Latin countries 'padre'. Only the Germans do not give their priests the attribute 'Father'. With the expression '*Herr* Pfarrer' the Germans see the priest as a member of the ruling class. The Germans were the nation which more than any other became a fatherless generation and which in autogenesis substituted the *Führer* for the father. Where the family is dissolved, and the role of the true father is taken over by a political father-figure society is sick. A father-figure is like the cruel god of the Greek myth who devours his own children.

Freud spent the first four years of his life in Freiburg (Bohemia). There the Jews lived in their still unbroken medieval piety, and there was no Jewish household into which the Day of Atonement with its atmosphere of a *mysterium tremendum* did not penetrate. Freud had the same childhood surroundings in the Jewish districts of the Vienna of the 1860s. Whatever the Freud family may tell Mr. Ernest Jones about Freud's freethinking father, even the most assimilated Jew of those days did not and could not free himself from the great power of the Day of Atonement. Even if it was only the solemn tune in which a cantor sang or a layman hummed the prayer '*Avinu Malkeinu*', 'Our Father, our King', the child Sigmund Freud was reached by this prayer, and even if he forgot it later, it rested in his subconscious mind.

Our Father, our King. But where was there for Freud a father whom he could respect? His father was of the Micawber type, always expecting that something would turn up, and always unable to save his family from grinding poverty. At the age of ten or twelve Freud was walking with his father when the latter told him of an incident of the past. The incident should prove that Jews were now living in happier days. As a young man Freud senior had been walking along the streets in Freiburg. He was well dressed and wore a fur cap. A Christian came along, knocked his cap into the mud and shouted: 'Jew, get off the pavement.' Anxiously the son asked the father: 'And what did you do?' He never forgot the calm reply: 'I went into the street and picked up the cap.' Sigmund Freud's future hero was the Semitic general, Hannibal, who hated Rome and almost destroyed it. Rome represents both political and religious authority, the authority of the Caesar and the authority of the popes. 'If Freud did not regard religious people as his enemies, we can be certain he did not look upon them as his friends,' writes G. L. Philp commenting on Freud's childhood reminiscence (*Freud and Religious Belief*, Rockliff, London, p. 20). But this reminiscence also throws some light on Freud's relationship with his father. Did he, could he respect him? 'Our Father, our King' – was there fatherhood, either in his own family, or in his generation, which could be revered according to the commandment: 'Honour thy father and thy mother, that thy days may be long upon the land which the Lord thy God giveth thee.'?

And was there in Freud's days a king to be revered as the holder of the office of David, the saviour of his people? There was the Emperor Franz Josef: The Viennese sang: '*Draussen im Schönbrunner Park sitzt ein alter Herr – sorgenschwer. Guter, lieber, alter Herr, mach' dir doch das Herz nicht schwer!*' (Yonder in the Park of Schönbrunn, sits an old man, full of sorrows. Dear, good old man, do not worry so much!). Here we have the blueprint of the myth-maker Freud. He had a vision – 'I would rather say vision, – not hypothesis', says he himself (*Autobiographical Study*, Hogarth Press, p. 124) 'that "in the beginning" people lived in hordes under the domination of a single powerful male.' 'One day, however, the sons came together and united to overwhelm, kill, and devour their father ...' (ibid. 124–5).

The prophets of old announced the coming of a day, a day of judgment, a *dies irae*, a terrible day still in the future but visible to them in the present. Freud also spoke of 'a day', a terrible day, the day of patricide. The 'day' of which he spoke as the primeval beginning of all history was in fact his own present. The weak king assaulted by the young sons of the 'hordes' was there in contemporary history. Freud saw and heard the 'hordes' from the window of his flat in *Berggasse*. The nationalism of the intellectuals had in his days become mass nationalism. The intellectuals had as historians, philologists and romantics discovered the new nationalities but lost the leadership of the nations to the politicians of the mass age. From his window Freud saw the Czechs demonstrating and demanding Czech schools in Vienna, he saw the demonstrations of German-speaking Austrians demanding that Vienna must remain German, he saw the demonstrations of the antisemites occupying the entrance to the university – situated only five minutes away from his flat – and preventing any Jew, or as the case might be, any member of the non-German nationalities – from entering the building. Finally he saw the marching columns of workers, led either by Social Democrats or by Christian-Socialists.

Freud would not dismiss his myth of the primeval hordes despite all the scholars who told him that he was talking nonsense. He saw what he saw and wrote about it. He wrote about the primeval hordes. He saw them from his window. And the father to be killed by his sons? In Schoenbrunn sits an old man, troubled by his sorrows. A quarter of an hour's walk from him sat a Russian, a tenant in his single room, studying Marx. His name was Stalin. A tramp with the name of Adolf Hitler strolled through the streets. Freud's 'vision' of a prehistoric past with wandering hordes and with a rebellion of sons who killed their father was a vision not of the past but of a future which he saw coming towards himself and his generation. It was a future which befell Europe where people had ceased to pray, 'Our Father, our King'. Freud was haunted by the vision of a fatherless generation. He had the vision, but he did not understand his own vision.

Freud was not a prophet, because his vision did not

place him outside the multitude for which it would have been a saving message. He was himself a part of this multitude, part of a fatherless generation. A fatherless generation dissolves itself into warring groups: brothers become enemies, nation fights against nation, and ploughshares are forged into swords. Being a Jew, this conflagration outside took place in his own heart. The hated father was everybody who belonged to the decadent establishment represented by 'the old man in Schönbrunn', his own father included. In his subconscious life Freud was assailed by self-hatred. Jewish self-hatred became common in a Jewish generation at the historical juncture when the westernised group of the Jewish people had to overcome the medieval form of life of the not yet westernised group. Jews also became 'hordes', sons who hated their fathers.

Freud was in the grip of what is now called by a freer Jewish generation 'Jewish self-hatred'. Only if we cease, when speaking of Jewish self-hatred, to imply that it is nothing but the neurotic and ignominious approach of the Jew to himself shall we have achieved mental freedom. We shall then have truly emancipated ourselves from our fascination with progress which is blind to the past, and from the psychological evils of persecution. History is not an organic process. History does not move on with the innocence and inevitability of the growth which takes place in nature. History is often a chain of tragic events. The past does not fall away from us like the slough of a snake. A struggle has to be fought to overcome or to preserve the past; a struggle has to be fought to bring forth a desired future or to prevent an unwanted one. Nothing happens organically in history, everything in history is brought into being by love or by hatred, by justice or by anarchy, by mercy or by cruelty, by truth or by folly.

The move away from the Middle Ages which had their sunset in Austria-Hungary was passionately desired by newborn nations and was stubbornly opposed by the old establishment, especially by the Roman Catholic Church. The Jews

who were attacked from the pulpit by the Roman Catholic
priests of the Christian-Socialist party were themselves
weighed down by the Middle Ages in their outmoded way
of life. The split into progressives and conservatives, as it
happened in Christian society, took place in the Jew himself.
The Jew, progressing from a past age into a new one, was
a man who both hated and loved a part of his own life.
Lovingly looking towards a future which emancipation and
westernisation held out for him, he could not but hate everything which prevented him from reaching the New Dawn.
But his hatred concerned his own Jewish past and was therefore self-hatred, because his past had formed him in his
'mother's womb' (Jeremiah i,5). This was all the more the
case the less he understood his past.

It was Zionism which cured the Jews of Austria-Hungary
of Jewish self-hatred. They never had the benefit of a Jewish
Reform Movement which mostly flourished among the German Jews and enabled them to reach inner human freedom
in the times of transition. The Zionist achievement of eman-
cipating Jews from an inferiority complex leading to self-
hatred may one day be regarded as equally important with
its political success. Looking back to Freud's Vienna we must
not speak with contempt of these Jewish writers and intellectuals who were in the grip of Jewish self-hatred. The way
to freedom is a long way. There are many pilgrims who
become sick and many do not reach the goal. The final word
about Jewish self-hatred has to come from an understanding
of the modern Jew, swayed by an inner struggle; two civilisations, the medieval and the modern, oppose each other
in the very self of the Jew. The conflict between westernised
Jews and Eastern European Jews has nothing to do with
the East-West conflict of today which is a conflict between
Asia and the West. The Eastern European Jew was himself
a westerner. His language was western – Yiddish is middle
high German. The secular part of his Polish culture was also
western. Poland was as Roman Catholic as any Latin nation.
The Eastern European Jew was a western Jew, but on a

medieval pattern. His fellow-Jews in Germany had emancipated themselves from the Middle Ages, and the Austrian
Jews were in the middle of this process. Torn between two
worlds, the modern Jew, outwardly diseased by self-hatred,
was again Jacob, the man who had to fight with God and
man, and even when achieving blessing in the end, left the
place of his struggle limping. The conflict between the
Middle Ages and the modern era was raging in the hearts of
individual Jews. The fate of the Jew and the fate of mankind are always inter-related. It was in Austria, among the
sick of a civilisation in travail, that the merciful healer
Sigmund Freud learnt his profession of psycho-analysis.

BOYS

The suicide in 1903 of the young Viennese Jew Otto Weininger at the age of twenty three proves that Zangwill's short story did not exaggerate the severity of the conflict between the not yet westernised father and his westernised son. Weininger as a person explains what kind of people Jewish writers like Karl Kraus and Franz Werfel and many others of this group around Freud were. Ludwig Wittgenstein, although different from them, belongs to them in more than one respect. Truly different from all of them is Franz Kafka. Freud wrote with admiration in his last book, 'Moses', of the Pharaoh Ikhnaton. The Egyptologists think little of this particular Pharaoh and call his age a 'butterfly age'. 'Today the impression that the art and civilisation of Amarna gives us is that of an ephemeral butterfly age with the total lack of moral standards usually associated with happy morons' (J. D. S. Pendlebury, Tell el-Amarna, p. 159–160). The Vienna of Freud with most of the Jewish writers, artists and philosophising physicians crowding round him was the home of a 'butterfly civilisation'. Rilke, not a Jew, was more representative of this civilisation than his Jewish fellow-writers and artists. He identified art with religion.

The Viennese Jewish *jeunesse dorée* did not go into the businesses of their successful fathers. They loathed the trades which provided the money which gave them independence and allowed them, if they wished, to live as playboys. Siegfrid Trebitsch, later famous as translator of G. B. Shaw's entire literary output, cut a ridiculous figure as a young man. He nearly died after a duel. The swords used in the duel were not lethal weapons. Under the code of the duel they could do no more than give with their possible cuts a martial appearance to a boyish face. But the sword of Trebitsch's opponent was rusty and our hero was laid up for weeks with blood-poisoning. During this time he was visited daily by the other young man, whose offence 'could only be washed away with blood'.

The non-Jewish, well-to-do-sons of imperial Vienna had the opportunities of the army, the higher civil service, and the Church. For the Jewish youth who had talent, character and ambition, art and science provided the way away from the reality in which they were born and bred. The Viennese medical faculty became world famous and was *verjudet,* full of Jews. Freud never considered baptism, which would have made his university career easier. He was an uprooted Jew. The Jewish scientists, artists and writers were reminded by the antisemites that they, who cared little or not at all about their Jewish faith, were still Jews. Their Jewish origin became their hated past. Some emphasised their Jewish existence as national characteristics and became Zionists, some suppressed it and became what the new terminology called 'assimilationists'. To Freud Jewish religion was a non-rational component of his life, unacknowledged, no longer understood, suppressed, but unpleasantly interfering with his daily existence.

Otto Weininger committed suicide because he hated his human existence as a Jew with the fierceness of an antisemite. He saw the two worlds, the Jewish world and the world which he admired, the ideal world created by artists and great politicians. The approaching end of the decaying Austrian Empire was not visible to Weininger. In the Vienna Opera he revelled in the works of Wagner, he revered Beethoven. The works of Goethe and Shakespeare were his Holy Scripture. The officers of the Hapsburgs in their impressive uniforms appeared to be heroes. An ideal world was not an illusion, it was there in contemporary history. Reality, as far as it was not affected by the ideal superstructure, was contemptible. Reality could be called, in the vein of Schopenhauer's idealism, 'Jewish', the attribute used with the

venom of the antisemite. Schopenhauer's indictment: 'reality
– a Jewish conception', hit out against Christianity, too. He
saw in the existence of the Jews a Christian meaning: the
Christian saint represents the homeless Jew, the talmudic
scholar studying his huge volumes, represents 'Jerome in his
cell'. Superficial comparative religion does not reveal much.

Weininger, although an expert in modern science, was
a medievalist. In medieval society there was no place for
two kinds of human beings: women and Jews. They were
regarded as contemptible. Weininger wrote a book called *Sex
and Character* in which he accepted the medieval scale of
values. He proves 'scientifically' the inferiority of women,
and as to the Jewish case he drew the same conclusion.
He went to an exhibition of Beethoven manuscripts, and in
this place, exalted in his eyes through the relics of the great
master, he shot himself. There were many candidates for a
suicide with Weininger's motive, but they lived to old age.
Freud was one of them. He never repudiated Judaism. He
can even be called a 'proud Jew'. But he was not free from
Jewish self-hatred which also tormented Marx and Lassalle.
When fourteen years old, Lassalle wrote in his diary: 'Two
types I hate – the Jews and the journalists.' And yet he also
wrote: 'I would risk my life in order to save the Jews from
their present oppressed situation. I would not even be
frightened by the guillotine, if I could make the Jews a
respected nation. Following up the trend of my childish
dreams, it is my dearest wish to lead the Jewish people,
a weapon in my hand, towards independence.'

Marx and Freud were throughout their lives different
from Lassalle. 'Marx and Freud have been called two of the
most terrifying antisemites' (*Stimmen der Zeit*, Vol. 148,
1951). Marx called Lassalle a *Judenjunge* (Jew boy). But
Bismarck said that any squire could be happy to have Lassalle
as his neighbour. 'Marx and Freud desired to be ultra Greeks
... and they succeeded in this endeavour to a surprisingly high
degree.' 'In the Jewish antisemite antisemitism becomes a
religious power. The Jewish antisemite wrestles with himself.

Marx abolished the Jew' (ibid.). Freud 'killed' his own father by inventing the myth of patricide, the father of the horde murdered by his sons. His last publication could have been written by any antisemitic Old Testament scholar.

Otto Weininger would have liked to be an ultra Greek. History was to him the glittering world of the sons, but not of Jewish sons. The Austrian officer-class, gay and idle, as they appear in Lehar's operettas, the Court, the Wagnerian theatrical Middle Ages of Parsifal, the music of Beethoven and Schubert, art and heroism – this was history, a world of gods and heroes. The Jewish world, as Anton Kuh, a gifted writer of the Viennese circle around Freud, describes it, is a world of 'old men with patriarchal caps, of parents, uncles and aunts'. It is a life lived in the family, centred round a table on which food is offered and where ceremonies are performed. A Jew, says Kuh, sees in the Jew 'a fellow-eater and a fellow-worshipper'.

The table at which the family in a Jewish home sits is indeed an altar. Jews do not have their altar in the Synagogue; they have it in their home. Freud refers to the Holy Communion of Christian worship when he talks about the totem meal. Of the Holy Communion in the Christian divine service Freud had no personal experience. Kuh's formula 'fellow-eater and fellow-worshipper', on the other hand, describes exactly Freud's childhood experience in which a father or a grandfather – Freud's grandfather had the title rabbi – sanctified a sabbath or festival meal in the ceremony of the *kiddush*. A Jewish code concerning Jewish ceremonials has the title *shulchan aruch,* which means, 'The properly laid table'. Any Jew, even the most assimilated, knows the two Hebrew words: *Shulchan aruch.* They also occur in the daily talk of a Jew who may not know any Hebrew. Freud, without any doubt, knew this expression. It meant to him something crude and primitive. How could he, the Jew ignorant of Judaism, know that the expression 'the laid table' is a quotation from Psalm 23 'Thou preparest a table before me in the presence of mine enemies'? Eating and worship-

ping together meant something primitive to the author of
Totem and Taboo. Had he really read the Bible, as he
claimed, he would have known that the numerous sacrifices
in the Hebrew Bible create communion with God during a
meal: God is our host, and we are his guests. Freud leaves
God out and sees a primitive custom. With God seen as
present, invoked as present at the meal, the custom even of
a primeval clan is not primitive, but is in all its simplicity
sublime.

A great Viennese rabbinic scholar whom Freud's father
would have had the knowledge to appreciate, is called by
Freud the son 'a very hard, bad, and uncouth man' (*Briefe*
1873–1939. Fischer Verlag, Frankfurt, 1960, No. 58). It is
worth while looking nearer to find out who was this man
who seemed to Freud so despicable. He was a lecturer at the
Viennese Rabbinic Seminary, the author of a standard work
on the oral rabbinic tradition, which even today is not dated
(*Dor, dor vedorshav*). His name was J. H. Weiss. On his
retirement, at the age of eighty, he concluded his manifold
scholarly publications with an autobiography which remains
an important source-book for the talmudic education in the
yeshivot of Bohemia during the time of his youth. This
autobiography also gives us a description of the life of Freud's
ancestors. We read there indirectly, but with cogent details,
of the life of Freud's grandfather and great-grandfather. Of
J. H. Weiss Sigmund Freud's letter speaks in a most dis-
respectful way: 'In his home there was no love but bitter
poverty, no culture but numerous duties.' All the sons had
to study 'in order to satisfy the great vanity of the father'.
In fact, none of the sons had a successful life – Freud's
letter tells us – and two of them committed suicide. One
of these unhappy sons was a medical colleague of Freud,
and Freud went to his funeral. The education of sons according to out-dated methods in the country of the *Kleine Nacht-
musik* could only have disastrous results. But Freud did not
learn the lesson which his observation of the tragedies in
the family of J. H. Weiss could have taught him. He merely

reacted to J. H. Weiss the father with the hatred which he as a son, unknown to himself, felt against his own father and which many westernised sons in Vienna, also unknown to themselves, felt against their own fathers.

Can a Jew get away from his Judaism? Weininger said no and shot himself. Freud did not shoot himself but found relief in another way. He rationalised his self-hatred by showing that it is a primitive sphere where fathers rule over sons. If the rule of the father was the order of the primitive sphere, he, the westernised, the emancipated son had no longer anything to do with it. The son had emancipated himself from the father. The Jew was no longer a Jew.

When Otto Weininger committed suicide, Karl Kraus was twenty-nine. He defended Weininger's death as a meaningful action which, he pleaded, the contemporary historical situation could not afford to ignore. Kraus was the greatest figure of the Viennese circle around Freud. From Freud's psycho-analysis Kraus kept aloof: 'I do not want to meddle in my private affairs.' Kraus acknowledges that man's mind has its inner experience which should remain his 'private affair'. This made him the creator of profound poems and essays. Kraus as editor of the *Fackel* was as well known in Vienna as Socrates was in Athens. Socrates said 'know thyself'. So did Freud. Kraus also said it, but said it as a satirist, as a relentless critic, as a pamphleteer.

His *Fackel*, like Maximilian Harden's *Die Zukunft* in Berlin, followed the example of Henri Rochefort's *La Lanterne*. Victor-Henri de Rochefort-Lucay (1831–1913) became the formidable opponent of Napoleon III. Rochefort had chosen the title *La Lanterne* for his journal because he wanted to remind his fellow citizens that during the French Revolution the aristocrats were hanged on lanterns. With his title *Die Fackel* Kraus followed no such programme. Politically, Kraus was a conservative. He attacked not a system but men, especially servile journalists and, regarding their sloppy language as a sin against the Holy Ghost, he called these *journaille*. In Viennese slang the word *canaille* was

54

used by the man in the street. Today we know the journalist
as a reporter, whose opportunities of making policy are
strictly limited. It was different in Karl Kraus' days. Jour-
nalism was a part of literature, and the journalists had access
to the corridors of power. It was said that in the office of
the mighty editor of the *Neue Freie Presse,* Moritz Benedict,
Balkan kingdoms were created and brought to nought. As
the *journaille* contained a high percentage of Jews, Kraus'
crusade against them was made passionate through his own
Jewish self-hatred.

The Spanish inquisitors investigated cases of Marranos,
of newly and superficially baptised Jews, and found the
criminal *opiniones Judaicae* in remarks which seemed of no
importance to the victims. Like these inquisitors Karl Kraus
persecuted his Jewish fellow writers and found Yiddish hidden in their German, and even exaggerated their style by
repeating it in Yiddish diction like an antisemite from the
gutter. He often had a case. The antisemitic journalist Stapel
found that Jews write either better or worse than the German
writers, but never like them. Buber, who in his old age called
himself a Polish Jew, wrote in a German style, both famous
and peculiar. Franz Rosenzweig, like no other German writer,
could still after World War I write German which was the
German of Goethe. But an age consists of the few who
are great and the many who are not great but have their
place and their function in contemporary literature. Those
who were not great are forgotten today, and one wonders
whether Karl Kraus' crusade against them was worthwhile.
Why did they annoy him so much? The answer is clear.
They were Jews, and he, the baptised Jew, had remained
a Jew. His Jewish self-hatred was alive, or shall we say
creative, in his literary criticism. Karl Kraus was the most
typical representative of Jewish antisemitism, and he was
also its most typical victim. He was forced to write, daily,
from morning till evening. When a newspaper reprinted an
essay of his but put a comma in the wrong place he went
to court because of it. He won his case. Is this greatness or

madness or both? Kraus wrote in self-defence against anybody who might have said, not even in words, but with a
look, in an innocent remark: 'You are a Jew.' This remark
was offensive, as it was said to one who knew nothing of the
holy glory of being a Jew.

One thing was common to the *Lanterne* and the *Fackel*.
Both journals refused to accept advertisements in order to
preserve their independence. Rochefort was not interested
in what was Karl Kraus' main purpose. Kraus wanted to save
the language from becoming soulless, dishonest and dead.
This puts him side by side with the linguistic philosophers
Ferdinand Ebner, Franz Rosenzweig, Ludwig Wittgenstein
and Heidegger. Freud also belongs to this group. He, too,
was deeply concerned with the word spoken by man. Its
subconscious meaning should be discovered, made conscious
and become fit for communication.

There are two sentences in Franz Rosenzweig's *Stern der
Erlösung* which provide the creative vision for the various
forms of linguistic philosophy, however different they eventually became. Rosenzweig writes 'The ways of God and the
ways of man are different, but the word of God and the
word of man are identical... What man hears in his heart
as his own human language is the word which comes from
the mouth of God.' Here the Jew Franz Rosenzweig and
the Roman Catholic Ferdinand Ebner are in full agreement.
Wittgenstein would have understood Rosenzweig whose
linguistic philosophy I venture to sum up in the words:
'Listen, O man: Listen to what a husband says to his wife,
a wife says to her husband, to what parents say to their
children and children say to their parents, what the bridegroom says to his bride, and the bride says to her bridegroom! Listen to what man says to his fellow-man. Listen
to the words once spoken and afterwards written down in
Holy Scripture. Listen, and you will hear the word of God
spoken by man.'

Rosenzweig turns to the private language of man and to
the Hebrew Bible. In these two instances he finds the word

which is still human because it is unaffected by the language of the advertisements and the bellowing of the puppets of the totalitarian age. Rosenzweig began to translate the Hebrew Bible into German. He was convinced, as the authors of the Septuagint were before him, that the Hebrew Bible can be translated into the language of western man. A decayed language can in this way be regenerated and can announce a message beginning with the words: 'Thus says the Lord.' The biblical prophet speaks his own word, and it is the word of God. The prophet, being not merely the mouthpiece of his own civilisation, speaks a word valid for all civilisations. In this he is not a superman but truly human.

Both Freud and Karl Kraus turned to words spoken by man. To Freud words were important because of their roots in the unconscious, to Karl Kraus words were important as the currency of culture. It can be argued that Freud made an important contribution to linguistic philosophy (of which he had no concept). He did so as the prophetic interpreter of words which cannot be understood if taken only as coming from the rational level of mind. Freud is more Jewish than Kraus who is mainly concerned with the cultural superstructure above reality.

The Empire decays because people write bad German: this is Karl Kraus' linguistic philosophy in a nutshell. Kraus remained a worshipper of culture, of great works of art, of poetry. He remained chained to aesthetic values. He was an uprooted Jew. He, who did not understand the biblical prophets, could not understand that in speech – as in love – the difference between transcendence and immanence disappears. Love and speech are immanent in man, and, at the same time, they transcend man. A word spoken by man, understood as the word of God, made the biblical prophet a man to whom the people of Jerusalem listened.

The people of Vienna in the years of their 'butterfly civilisation' had no prophets, nor were they men of the kind which listens to prophets. This gap was filled by apostate Jews who, if they were not prophets, preached like Karl

57

Kraus. He preached as satirist, as critic, and as the evangelist of what is called today 'the new morality' of which he was the first immature pioneer.

Solitude was praised by Schopenhauer and Nietzsche, by Oscar Wilde, Baudelaire and Flaubert. It was recommended to youth as a situation offering creative possibilities. But which solitude, we must ask these men of the *fin de siècle*. To be alone is every man's predicament. It must be endured, and can be endured, without bitterness, and in a spirit which always looks for and finds human contacts. To be alone in the sense of being cut off is dangerous and has to be avoided. Boys who cut themselves off from their fathers and teachers when they have their first sexual awakening, and remain 'fixed' in this solitude, are condemned to remain boys for their whole lives. They may become poets and writers of a sort, even creators of great books, but men, adults, they will not become. Otto Weininger and Karl Kraus were helped financially by their loving Jewish fathers who were still alive when the two were boys. But the difference between westernised sons and not yet westernised fathers made the two 'fatherless'. Being fatherless they were not qualified to write about marriage and love. They wrote a lot about the emancipation of sexuality from prejudice. They could not help, because they themselves were in need of help. They were without help from their fathers when they had been boys and this condemned them to a long-drawn-out adolescence for life.

Freud – and also the playwright and novelist Arthur Schnitzler – remained aloof from Karl Kraus' propaganda for 'healthy sexuality'. Karl Kraus never realised that he was fighting a crusade against the Christian heresy of Manichaeism. Manichaeism equates sex and sin. Freud remained a physician. He grew into mature manhood, where others remained boys until their death in old age. Kraus remained an unmarried man making the Viennese *Kaffeehaus* his home. His 'affairs' were many, as his poems, some of lasting beauty, reveal. Freud lived as a *pater familias*.

Karl Kraus entered the Roman Catholic Church. In 1920 the Salzburg Cathedral and the Franciscan Church were allowed to be used as the backcloth for a performance of Hoffmansthal's *Jedermann* (Everyman). This enraged Karl Kraus and he rejoined the Jewish Community. He had aesthetic reasons for joining the Church and aesthetic reasons for leaving it. Christian faith has nothing to do with this kind of baptism. Nor is baptism as breakdown a true conversion to Christianity. Nietzsche wrote of Wagner: 'He broke down at the Cross'. Parsifal's faith, i.e. the faith of Wagner's Parsifal, is the end of a journey of despair and not the victory over despair. It is the same in Orwell's novel *1984* where the poor victim of cruel totalitarianism looks at Big Brother and imagines that he loves him.

About the baptism of Franz Werfel only rumours exist. In America he was often visited by a Roman Catholic priest who showed in various ways his kindness to the sick and down-and-out-refugee. If Werfel became baptised, of which fact no reliable record exists, it would have been a death-bed conversion, another case of one who 'broke down at the Cross'. More to the point is Werfel's approach to a Christian setting which he often chose in his writings. There is no real commitment to Christianity in his many references to the Christian faith, but it is not made clear that there is no commitment. His *Christozentrik* as 'source of rejoicing in existence' must be traced to Goethe, not to the New Testament. The worst example is his novel *The Song of Bernadette*. The reader is left to assume that the author shares Bernadette's belief in the miracle. But does he? If he does not, we must say that a Jewish author unable to accept the Christian faith wrote a book with the aim of edifying a Roman Catholic public. On the whole it is more his lack of proper knowledge in matters of Jewish and Christian theology than lack of character for which Werfel has to be blamed.

Henri Bergson and Edmund Husserl died as faithful Jews. The scraps of utterances collected by Christians, in-

terested in missionary work for Jews, (J. H. Oesterreicher:
The Walls are Crumbling, London 1953) prove nothing. The
two great philosophers died in a world echoing the victories
of Hitler. They did not die as Christians, but they felt they
had to die like the Christ of the New Testament. They spoke
like that in one way or another to the Roman Catholic
nursing sister and to the few friends who dared to come
and visit them. The one died in Paris, the other in Germany,
both deserted by former disciples and friends, cut off from
the world in which the heathen Caesar had triumphed. Both
refused to give in, and died as Jews.

We cannot say anything so noble about Werfel. But
we can defend him. 1937 in *Höret die Stimme* (Listen to the
Voice) he spoke against the times, whereas the Churches in
Austria went with the times. He was a novelist, a poet, and a
pamphleteer with a moral cause. Writing about the relationship between the Jewish and the Christian faith, he was
misinformed and muddled. It is strange that his *Paul amongst
the Jews* appeared in 1926, seven years after Franz
Rosenzweig had finished his *Stern der Erlösung* and six
years after its publication, and twenty years after Albert
Schweitzer's *The Quest for the Historical Jesus.* But Werfel,
like Freud, clung to the views of the Victorian scholars who
ignored the Jewish roots of Christianity in the ages before
Paul.

Simone Weil wrestled with Christianity and died a
Jewess. She did not become baptised. There was no Simone
Weil in Freud's Vienna. What Freud and Werfel wrote about
Paul – let everyone who studies Freud be warned! – is historical and theological nonsense. The Church in Austria was
not in a position to give an impressive account of herself
and in this way to challenge Jews to respond with a profound
testimony to Judaism. Buber, who originally belonged to the
Vienna of Freud and Karl Kraus, left it, settled near Frankfurt, studied philosophy which Freud as a positivist avoided
like the plague, and, joining Franz Rosenzweig, saved his
soul. Yet in the fine art of his short essays, Buber is a

pupil of Kraus. All his life Buber adhered to his belief in
the concept of a 'Jewish culture'. Culture, the aesthetic
substitute for Church, religion and, indeed, for God, was the
centre of Viennese humanism. Against this humanism
Grillparzer, with whom Karl Kraus is often compared as
a writer, had warned his fellow Austrians with the words:
'From humanism to nationalism, from nationalism to barbarism.' With his message of Jewish culture, preached in
various forms, Buber remained a man of the Vienna circle.

A generous postscript has to be written about the sad
chapter of the wave of baptisms in the Jewish bourgeoisie
and among the Jewish intellectuals. First of all, it happened
among a small minority. The Viennese Jewish population
turned away from these individual cases with contempt. They
regarded them as cowards. Not a single case can be shown
of a Jew conspicuous as a leading personality in the public
or literary life of Vienna becoming a Christian out of conviction. But numerous cases are known in which Jews at
the universities, in the civil service, in the army, threw away
advantages which baptism, explained to them as a formality,
would have granted.

The generous postscript to all this has to point out that
the Vienna of 1900 had become an island of positivism and
psychology, of the natural sciences and of music. Philosophy,
epistemology, critical thinking about thinking, was out, and
the enlightenment, not of the great Voltaire, but of the little
schoolmasters, was in. Freud was a typical example. He
wrote: 'Even when I have moved away from observation,
I have carefully avoided any contact with philosophy proper.
This avoidance has been greatly facilitated by constitutional
incapacity' (*An Autobiographical Study*, p. 109).

Franz Werfel's play *Paulus unter den Juden* (Paul
amongst the Jews), is written on the basis of the error which
contrasts Judaism as law with Christianity as love.
By that time Geiger and other German Jews had produced
works rehabilitating Pharisaic Judaism, so that the theological
antithesis between law and love was relegated to the armoury

of a backward Christian theology. Hermann Cohen and Franz Rosenzweig had published their works. Nothing of it penetrated Austrian Jewry. The orthodox rabbis objected to German-Jewish influence, as being 'neology', reform', the intellectuals without contact with rabbis had read Buber's immature *Reden über das Judentum* (Lectures about Judaism) and discussed Zionism. Religious Judaism interpreted in the language of the new age was not available for those Jews who would have liked to enter into a Jewish-Christian dialogue. Nowhere in Austria was there an opportunity for a Jewish-Christian dialogue. The confrontation was not between Jew and Christian, but between Jew and antisemite. The Christian priest was as a rule an antisemite. In this insincere, hateful, in fact godless atmosphere Jewish baptism was – a formality. The baptised Jew left his Jewish faith of which he did not know anything and entered Christianity of which he, being still a Jew under his skin, did not think much. Max Brod wrote a poem about the baptised Jews in which he ends with the self-accusation: 'We have not loved you enough.'

The baptism of Karl Kraus and Otto Weininger was not a real conversion. And yet, in their aesthetic preference for history, for superstructure above reality to reality itself, they were more Christians than Jews. In this respect Freud had nothing to do with the Viennese circle. His *Future of an Illusion* can be ignored as an attack on belief in God but must be carefully read as a criticism of established religion and of culture and civilisation.

Freud as the discoverer of the non-rational structure of the human mind drew a metaphysical conclusion about the nature of the universe. The world appeared to him in a way which man's visible and accountable history did not reveal. Speaking in theological terms, Freud defended the superiority of creation against history. He stands where before him stood Marx who rehabilitated the material world which was ignored and neglected by the spiritualistic Hegel. On behalf of Marx and Freud Simone Weil speaks the right word: 'The substance of matter is – obedience.' The sentence of this Jewish girl leads into the post-Marxist and post-Freudian age. The economic fate of man – the way our daily bread is providentially provided – elements of our thinking – the conditions of our belief in God – are mysteriously directed by the material world itself, by the subconscious layer of the human mind, by – Creation. Marx and Freud unmasked history. They were both Jews, and their contribution to mankind has to be gratefully acknowledged as a Jewish one. What the Marxists and the Freudians did with the revelation which the two pioneers were chosen to receive is not their fault. They were misunderstood, and they themselves, as can happen with prophets, did not clearly understand the consequences of their own vision.

They looked into history without illusion. They, and we, the generation after them, saw the face of Medusa. The face of a Saviour did not appear. This is the challenge of Marx and Freud to Christianity. Marx's and Freud's materialistic metaphysics is dead. But the challenge of Marx and Freud remains, it is a Jewish challenge, and Christianity has to answer it. We Jews wait for this answer which must come forward, if a Judaeo-Christian civilisation is to come again.

The Vienna circle, with its aesthetic belief in history, was a pre-Marxist and pre-Freudian last attempt to give history a meaning by proclaiming that art offers redemption. This is not true, although it has been naïvely believed in Europe since the Renaissance and, as hope against hope, alleged for the last time by such writers of despair as Stendhal, Flaubert and Nietzsche. The dying imperial Vienna gave the artist the function of entertaining a public, certain of the coming end and too feeble to master a tragic situation. The Viennese were fond of saying that their situation was 'desperate but not serious'.

The belief of the Renaissance that art is the highest value in man's life became a bourgeois prejudice and is today not even this. 'We have experienced that art . . . can also be a vice. Criminals can make use of it. Anyone not knowing this situation is a man of yesterday ... Beauty in itself is nothing, all depends on the man who creates it and on the reason why he creates it. Beauty is today the common possession of thousands. Thousands create it, thousands misuse it. Art even bores us, we no longer believe in art' (Walter Muschg: *Die Zerstörung der deutschen Literatur*, The Destruction of German Literature, Paul List Verlag, Munich).

The Jewish writers of the Vienna circle believed in art. When the catastrophe came they had nothing to say. Karl Kraus stopped publishing the *Fackel* in 1933. Hitler occupied Austria in 1938. Kraus, who died in 1936, would have had three years to find the right word against Hitler. His friends urged him to continue to publish his journal. He refused. He did not want to speak in the apocalyptic hour. His unwillingness was inability. It turned out he was, in the words of Nietzsche, 'only a fool, only a poet'. He had nothing of the prophet. He admitted *Mir fällt auf Hitler nichts ein* (I have nothing to say with regard to Hitler). He published, though, one heart-rending poem, *Letztes Gedicht* (Last Poem) in which millions who lived through the Hitler era will find their own mournful mood expressed:

> '... *No word is right*
> *One speaks only in one's sleep*' ...

It ends with the line:

> '*The word went to sleep* (entschlief – *died*)
> *when that world awakened.*'

In Germany Leo Baeck, Martin Buber and many rabbis could under the very noses of the Gestapo find words which reached their fellow Jews and the world. 'The word' did not go to sleep in German Jewry from 1933 to 1939. It may be that some of Buber's writings will one day become dated. What he wrote in Germany from 1933 to 1938 will last. In these writings Buber appears fully emancipated from his aesthetic Viennese beginnings. But Karl Kraus' silence must not only be judged as a negative attitude. The poet Kraus saw more clearly than did the psycho-analyst Freud. Freud had developed his psycho-analytical therapy into a psycho-analytical totalitarianism. This psycho-analytical totalitarianism, as it has been called, is no longer confined to psychology but makes metaphysical statements about man and his world. No wonder that Freud misjudged his time. The victory of Hitler in Germany in 1933 did not open Freud's eyes to the real situation. What he said in those years to his biographer Ernest Jones testifies to the shallowness of a bourgeois pre-occupied with his own position and pushing away from his own conscience the thought of mankind. Karl Kraus, at least, 'spoke' through his silence – though not by the spoken word – and impressively told of the imminence of the human catastrophe.

Vienna did not die when Hitler marched into the imperial city. But many Jews died, or were marked for death soon to come. They lived, when they were poor – and the majority was poor – in the district called *Leopoldstadt*. Those who could save themselves are now dispersed all over the world. What is Vienna today? It is the city of Freud even more than anything else. It is the city of the *Donauwaltzer*. A friendly city? The neolithic peasants of the Alpine villages which surround Vienna, the protoypes of Freud's 'hordes', who were held at bay during the reign of Franz Josef conquered through Nazism the city of writers, artists, musicians, scientists and humanists. The waltzing stopped, the lights of the ballroom went out. Nazism is more of Austrian than of German origin. The Austrian peasant population led by Roman Catholic clergy of peasant stock did not defend the city against the onslaught of the barbarians. Freud's vision of 'hordes' was reality. But the guilt of the worshippers of beauty must not be overlooked. As Grillparzer, a great Austrian, said, the way from the worship of beauty leads to the Beast of the Apocalypse.

Vienna was not Brecht's city of Mahagonny nor was it an innocent Nineveh, which deserved the mercy of God. It was a city in which Jews were killed, in that respect a city like others. Why do Christian people kill Jews? Why do

E   65

sons kill their fathers, as Freud tells us they do in the myth which he invented. Has the myth-maker Freud given his Jewish answer to the question, 'What is Christian history?'

Vienna was a city of ordinary people, Christians and Jews, w. ongly portrayed by Lehar and in 'La Ronde'. Jerusalem, when it was destroyed by Rome, was also a city inhabited by ordinary people. Holy events take place among ordinary people. To contemplate these holy events, to interpret them, gives us survivors consolation, guidance and the strength to hope again. There was Dr Johnson's London, Tolstoi's Moscow, Balzac's Paris, Fontane's Berlin, Joyce's Dublin. There was also Freud's Vienna. It died 1938.

But here it is again: Vienna 1967. Hard currency, good Viennese food, Opera and *Burgtheater;* people flock to the Prater, enjoy themselves in the Stadtpark, spend their Sundays in the Vienna Woods. The ashes of the murdered Viennese Jews are in Auschwitz amongst those of the six million. We Jews remember. What do we remember? We remember the destruction of Jerusalem. We remember history. It is not a place of salvation. That is the word of the Jew to the Christian. The destruction of Jerusalem is an historic event. It is a Jewish custom to say to a mourner: 'May the Lord comfort you with all those who mourn for Zion and Jerusalem.' Of history our view is not one of despair, but it is a mature view. History is not yet redeemed. Creation, on the other hand, is the source of our strength which destroys despair, and of our happiness: Creation – God saw what He had created, and behold, it was very good. The Jew, worshipping the Creator of the world in the family, and the Christian gentile, worshipping the saviour of history, are as different from each other as Jew and gentile, and as near to each other as brothers. When they talk to each other in peace, the world has peace.

THE PATRIARCH AND THE UNRULY SONS

Weininger was fascinated by the glitter of history. His vision was that of Richard Wagner. Weininger, who was baptised on the day on which he received his Ph.D. from Vienna University, and who committed suicide at the age of twenty three, was 'the boy who refused to grow up'. His dream was to be like one of the heroes of history. History was Valhalla. If, as a Jew, he was unfit to graduate to such a career in history, he preferred to die.

Karl Kraus was fascinated by the Holy Ghost in human language. The word in its cultural appearance, as written word, as literature, was either revelation of the holy spirit or blasphemy. He exorcised the blasphemy. He could achieve no more as a pioneer of linguistic philosophy. He revered the word, but recognised it only as the word spoken by man. That the word spoken by man can be the word of God, as his countryman Ebner and as Franz Rosenzweig realised, remained unknown to Karl Kraus. He was an atheist and insisted at the same time on the existence of Holy Scripture.

Freud was different from Weininger and Kraus who represent the many who belonged to the Vienna circle. In the midst of these Viennese men of letters and of the arts – some of them very gifted and still remembered, some only representing the spirit of the day in happy mediocrity – Freud stood like a sombre patriarch surrounded by unruly sons. The juxtaposition patriarch-son is not merely metaphorical language. We have learnt to introduce the terms patriarchal and matriarchal into the understanding of our modern social life. The patriarchal society or the patriarchal layer of society need not be situated in the primeval past. Our own society can, if necessary, be described as patriarchal or as matriarchal. The patriarchal type of man creates a world which we characterize as the world of the fathers, in which authority, stability, family life and the pursuit of the good life are

67

predominant. On the other hand, there is the world of the sons, in which not the hearth but the market place gives direction, in which life is not private but public, in which tragedy is faced by people creative in the arts and politics. In this Vienna circle of writers and artists a world of sons appeared on the stage. But Freud was not one of them. He was a patriarchal character. To use the word patriarchal to define the character of modern man may seem strange to those who are wont to hear the word in connection with Old Testament figures. Yet it is necessary to speak of Freud, the patriarchal figure.

There is no need to connect any dignity or even holiness with the character which the sociological type of the patriarch represents. One can admire the patriarchs of Genesis and then, speaking of the patriarchal type of Freud, say that he was not at all a warm or a lovable person, tyrannical in his family, and most thoroughly domineering in his relations with his colleagues. This is the picture which Erich Fromm gives us of Freud. It is a reliable picture. The fellow psycho-analysts and disciples, nearly all of them Jews, who disagreed with Freud were treated by him as heretics and deserters.

To understand Freud, one has to know something about the Czech village Jew in Freud, and I doubt whether his biographer Ernest Jones is capable of this understanding. How can he be? English Puritanism has a Mediterranean loveliness in comparison with the grimness of Jewish life in the small villages of Bohemia where the Jews found refuge after Maria Theresa's (1740–1780) persecution. The Jews living among the Czech peasants had to be tough to survive. The Middle Ages around them lasted up to 1848. The German which these Jews – and Freud – spoke had a harshness which made every German-speaking Czech, Gentile or Jew, recognisable as hailing from Bohemia. The sound of this German was quite different from the musical *Wienerisch* (Viennese idiom).

Kafka gives us an insight into the deep piety of the

Czech Jews in his short story *The Marten in the Synagogue*.
According to Jewish law a place of worship where an animal
has lived undisturbed, cannot be used as a synagogue. But
Kafka uses the presence of the animal in the synagogue as
his surrealist device to show the strong presence of the
mysterium tremendum in a wooden village synagogue. The
women sometimes see the marten crawling up the curtains
of the *Torah* shrine. They are so used to it that they cease
to be afraid. The men pray and no longer do anything
about the animal. It has become part of the place of worship.
Kafka, being Kafka, succeeds in re-creating the atmosphere
of such a village synagogue in which the poor Jews prayed,
while outside the enemy, the Christian, was lord. The Jews
prayed, and when they moved from the villages to the cities
and remembered their praying in the wooden synagogue, they
had a yearning to pray again in the same way as they had
prayed in the synagogue in which a *mysterium tremendum*
enveloped their worship. Such was the piety of the Czech
village Jews from whom Freud sprang. Their piety shaped
him, his atheism was a veneer.

Freud was an offspring of these tough and pious
'country' Jews. His grandfather and great-grandfather were
both learned, their grandchild Sigmund received from them
this heritage of toughness and intellectual agility. Should we
attribute it to stubbornness, narrow-mindedness or rather
toughness that Freud remained unmoved by the criticism
which his theory of the beginning of history, 'the father of
the horde killed by his sons', provoked from all quarters
of the world of learning? Freud supposed – wrongly – that
primeval man lived in hordes, each dominated by a powerful
male. 'The young males were forced out of the tribe to find
mates and the young females could expect no mate but the
leaders of the horde. This would obviously be a disagreeable
situation to both the young women and the young men of
the tribe. Freud suggested that the young men had in fact
risen in a body to murder their father and gain possession
of his women' (Stafford Clark, *What Freud Really Said*, p.

221). Ethnologists, anthropologists, archaeologists and biblical scholars all protested against this theory which, if it is called a myth, is a myth made up by Freud himself making use of material provided by Darwin. In spite of universal opposition, Freud did not give up his story of the 'beginning'. He changed what he had first regarded as fact into a 'hypothesis', and as he had to give up his story even as a 'hypothesis', he called it his 'vision'. As a visionary Freud has in this instance to be taken seriously. This has not yet been done. What is Freud's vision in his exposition of the beginning of civilisation, that is, of history?

Freud, in his criticism of religion, always speaks of the 'pious'. The great variety of the religious world is reduced to a world of the 'pious'. Who are they? Jews? Christians? Both? Freud did not yet live in an age in which comparative religion had widened the horizon of even ordinary people beyond Judaism and Christianity. The pious, as Jews, offered the westernised Jew a picture of a people mostly concerned with rituals. Freud took no account of the efforts of the German rabbis of the Reform Movement to distinguish between forms of religious life and the doctrinal essence of Judaism, to justify a withering away of certain ceremonials and to limit their former great number. The German-Jewish Reform Movement did not penetrate the Jewish communities of Austria. Freud, as an avowed atheist, did not feel any inclination to deal with his criticism of the ceremonials of the pious like a Jewish Reformer. His Jewish self-hatred, of which we have spoken above, excluded a positive attitude towards the specific Jewish religious problems of the modern age. His hostile preoccupation with the 'pious' turned, above all, to the Christians. When he left his flat in the Berggasse he stepped into the Christian world, and that meant into antisemitic Vienna, into a world of enemies. The Christians were the dangerous enemies. They threatened not only as a people of the gutter. Psycho-analysis was closely watched by the Roman Catholic Church and denounced as a Jewish science which the pious must avoid as a sinful heresy. Freud's view of religion was his view of Christianity, and as history and civilisation are shaped by Christianity, it was also his view of history and civilisation.

The patriarchal Jew Freud looked at history: What did he see? The home is a place of peace. The world outside the home knows only strife, discontent and war. When the inhibiting forces of civilisation are removed, we see men in their true light as 'savage beasts to whom the thought of sparing their own kind is alien'. This is the thesis of *The Future of an Illusion* and *Civilisation and its Discontents*. This thesis is that of Nietzsche, accepted by Hitler. Freud calls religion 'the universal obsessional neurosis of humanity' in which is perpetuated the illusion of a heavenly father who promises happiness in the hereafter in return for the renunciation of instinctive desires on earth. We need only substitute the word 'Christianity' for 'religion' to see the identity between Freud and Nietzsche. But Freud did not draw the consequences which Nietzsche drew. He remained a Jew with his contempt of violence; whatever his beliefs about God, man and the world were, he demanded justice between man and man in political and private affairs. The sons may be unruly, but that cannot make the government of the patriarch anything but moral government. Freud's moral *postulata* and his myth of the primordial patricide contradict each other blatantly.

Patricide was the key to Freud's understanding of history. It was, of course, a Jewish understanding which Freud, ignorant of any theological knowledge of Judaism and Christianity, drew from the subconscious layer of his mind. When he told the story of patricide, his Jewish ancestors spoke. He, Freud was a Jew, he knew that the sons who threatened his patriarchal existence were the Christians. The two brothers Tharaud, excellent writers with a sociological understanding, give us a picture of a Jewish childhood in Czechoslovakia. When the Jewish children saw a cross at the road side – and there were many in this Roman Catholic country – they ran away, terror stricken, as if harm could

71

be done to them at any moment by the man on the cross. The adults were also disposed to see the Cross as not different from the Arch of Titus. *Judaea capta – vae victis!* This world shaped the subconscious mind of Freud, who regarded his vision of the sons killing the father as meaningful, nay, as the truth about the beginning of history. It was the vision of a patriarchal Jew.

Freud could not lead his fatherless generation back to the understanding of fatherhood. Kafka could do it. His *Letter to my Father* shows the difference between them. Freud is the seer who has the vision but does not understand his own vision. It is the vision of a society which is neither political nor spiritual. Besides State and Church mankind is offered a third social possibility.

Christianity is sociologically a fraternity. Democracy as fraternity reveals its Christian roots. Democracy was established through regicide. The Church is the brotherhood of the sons who as sons are not what fathers are. The profligate son returns to his father, but his status as son remains different from the patriarchal status. We face in the sociological status of sonship the human person active outside the home. The Church is brotherhood, there is no difference between father and son, no difference between Greek and barbarian, master and slave. They are at one in the brotherhood of the sons. The brotherhood expiates the guilt of the sons who have left the fathers. The Church expiates the patricide of the beginning.

The State, too, begins its history with a guilt. The State creates stability through justice. But here, in the political sphere, justice could only be established by the application of power. Every political society has a skeleton in the cupboard: an *arreton,* as the Greek called it, something unspeakable, a guilt.

Patricide and regicide, and therefore deicide, is the guilt of the sons. The history of gentile and Christian starts with a guilt. The jubilant cry of Genesis i, 1 is: 'In the beginning God created heaven and earth'. Part of this guiltless reality is the home of patriarchal man. In the home the family lives in the innocence of Adam and Eve and in the peace which man in history will taste in the light of messianic salvation, and that will happen, according to Jewish teaching, 'at the end of days'.

In the post-Constantinian Christian era, in the era when the union of State and Church ends under the impact of the third social possibility, there is besides State and Church the society which is not political and not spiritual but has the reality of a household. Its basis is more economical than political, as Marx realised. Its spiritual elements have their roots in a subconscious layer of the mind, as Freud realised. Marx and Freud regarded the material world as different from what was only history, only superstructure, they discovered Creation, the world created not by man. Social life, rising from economic conditions, leads nearer to the created world than do political and spiritual forms of life. In our post-Constaninian era the State is inadequate for the needs of the coming age which is already present. The State cannot unite the great human family of the globe. To the word 'State' and to the word 'Church' a third word is now required to name the new form of human living-together. It seems that this third word, coined by Hegel, is society (see pp. 62/63).

Freud and Marx were the firm, though inadequate, prophets of the society in which the economic problems and the non-rational frame of the human mind are not neglected, and in which man's home is not restricted by a territory but has its place everywhere on the globe. In this new world which stretches over the whole creation, sons cannot rule alone. A return to the fatherhood as the holy office of man has to be comprehended. With the pursuit of human society which is neither political nor spiritual society, we need not advocate anti-statism – often necessary against some of our nation states – nor need we look with hostility to the Churches. But we must prepare for a social life which is in many respects a new life. In this new life the faith established by the fathers is not eliminated by the faith established by the sons.

IN THE BEGINNING

Heinrich Heine's poem *Die Lorelei* is a romantic poem. It speaks of 'a fable dating from *uralten Zeiten*' (from time immemorial). Professor A. Leschnitzer in his excellent study *Der Gestaltwandel Ahasvers* (Zwei Welten, Tel Aviv, 1962) reminds us that this fable, supposed to have been preserved from prehistoric times, was, in fact, non-existent before 1820. Then it was published by Clemens Brentano. So Brentano is the author of the fable which Heine in his immortal poem calls a tale from *uralten Zeiten*. A myth was born in the midst of contemporary history. A man whose life we know in all its details from birth to death stands before us as a myth-maker.

The antisemitic myth of Ahasuerus, too, was created in the full light of the nineteenth century. In the Middle Ages and in the age of the Reformation the legend of Ahasuerus did not have an antisemitic bias, but was a religious parable of a man to whom the Christian redemption of 'blissfully dying' was denied. The nineteenth-century myth of Ahasuerus was something else and something new. Gentiles and Jews united to remake the myth. It lost its religious content and received a political meaning. Leon Pinsker, the forerunner of Herzl, demands in his book *Auto-Emancipation* (1882) that the Jewish people should stop being the Ahasuerus among the gentiles, the wandering Jew without a home of his own. Heine, the German emigrant living in France, broods about his life without a fatherland and calls it the life of Ahasuerus. Boerne is annoyed and troubled about the pre-occupation with the Jew, displayed in Frankfurt in the press and in gossip. The gentiles see the Jew as a ghost whom they imagine as turning up always and everywhere. They see him, Boerne says, as an Ahasuerus.

To these authors of the myth of Ahasuerus Professor Leschnitzer adds the entire German bourgeoisie as co-authors. The German bourgeoisie was distressed about the failure of the Revolution of 1848. They had won no political victory over the feudal class, but the Jews had gained economic advantages. This grudge of the bourgeoisie against the Jews originated in the age of the Nation-States. Ahasuerus began to represent the Jewish nation to the gentiles. Nations come and go. The Jewish people remains, and this is seen as a curse by the disciple of Schopenhauer, Richard Wagner, who depicts the Nibelungen-end for his own German people in his *Götterdämmerung.* Wagner joins the others and gives the final touch to the nineteenth-century myth of Ahasuerus by writing in *Judentum in der Musik* (Judaism in Music) (1850): 'Remember, only one possibility exists for you (the Jew) to rid yourself of the curse which is on you: the redemption of Ahasuerus – the end, death.'

Weininger, the gifted, noble, misguided Jewish boy took Wagner's advice and committed suicide. What about Freud? In *The Future of an Illusion* he deals with religion generally. But what lesson would a Jewish reader learn from Freud? Could he not, as a Jewish reader, see his master in agreement with Richard Wagner, who saw the solution of the Jewish question in the disappearance of the Jew? And could not a Christian reader find in Freud's theory of religion similar advice for himself: progress towards true humanity through the abolition of the Christian faith? How distressing and terrifying to see the Jew Sigmund Freud and Adolf Hitler in agreement that a Judaeo-Christian *Weltanschauung* has to disappear!

The nineteenth-century mythmaker comes forward when the images of the Bible lose their impact on man. What was there in the beginning? The answer can be given by the historian or by the scientist of the evolutionary school. The trouble is that we often get answers from scholars who are historians stepping into the science of evolution or from scientists dealing with evolution but offering historical facts.

What is neglected is a clear distinction between history and development. In nature we observe development: caterpillar becomes butterfly. History is the place where a break in the chain of development occurs, where something new happens. In history we can speak of beginning, whether it can be chronicled or not. In science the mere assumption of a beginning is unscientific. Behind every discovered stage of nature the scientist must search for a preceding stage.

Freud received his theory of the beginning of religion from Robertson Smith's *The Religion of the Semites*. With this theory 'not much was lacking to enable me to recognise the killing of the father as the nucleus of totemism and the starting point in the formation of religion' (Freud: *An Autobiographical Study*, pp. 123–124). Robertson Smith only guesses about the early beginning of Semitic history, about which we know nothing. His theory was in no way historical, but it was an evolutionary theory like all the anthropological theories of the time. 'The evolutionary bias is conspicuous throughout, and is particularly clear in his (Robertson Smith's) insistence on the materialistic crudity – what Preuss called *Urdummheit* – of primitive man's religion, thus placing the concrete, as opposed to the spiritual, at the beginning of development' (Evans Pritchard, *Theories of Primitive Religion*, Clarendon Press, Oxford 1965, pp. 52–53).

We can fully endorse Evans Pritchard's criticism of Freud. Freud is indeed the scientist who deems himself permitted to make historical and indeed metaphysical statements on the basis of his evolutionary theory. But one postscript is necessary to this criticsm. Freud is not only the naïve scientist neglecting the simplest warning of epistomology, he is also the Jew who is restrained in the face of the category of the spiritual. Holy and profane are the categories of the Old Testament, spiritual and secular those of the New Testament. Freud's indictment of 'illusion' is his rejection of a spiritual realm regarded as wholly identical with the world of religion.

Besides his negative attitude to what the Christian calls spiritual and afterwards values as holy, because it is, first of all, spiritual, Freud has a further conviction which distinguishes him as a Jew from the Christian. Freud stresses the social character of early religion. Preference for social characteristics, together with a reserved attitude to personal characteristics, is strong in Freud. In these likes and dislikes we hear the voice of the Jew going back to the deepest layer of his subconscious experience of past ages. Freud is here not even a Jew shaped by the rabbinical interpretation of the Old Testament, but a Jew shaped by the Old Testament itself.

Freud thinks that he is a scientist, whereas he leaves science far behind and becomes as a myth-maker a metaphysician. To offer a theory about the beginning of man, of language, of history is to make metaphysical statements. It was not in the least Freud's intention to enter metaphysics. He regarded himself a scientist of the positivist school. His metaphysical statements are made in the naïvety of a belief which regarded them as scientific, as statements derived from 'logical analysis'. Freud failed to realise that man can have knowledge which is not scientific and yet capable of rendering truth. With his determined intention to avoid philosophy he plunged into a philosophy without the critical apparatus accessible to the post-Kantian philosopher.

The scientist cannot by-pass the joy of the Psalmist. This joy is a fact confronting the comprehending mind of scientist and popular observer alike. The joy about the creation of the world, of man, of language reveals facts as true as anything which science observes although they are not derived by science.

Freud insists that what is not scientific knowledge is, if not error, illusion. But scientific method entangles itself in what Kant calls 'antinomies'. The world has a beginning – the world has no beginning, is the first of the antinomies. Antinomies are contradictions which human reason observes as contradictions but which it is unable to solve. No myth-

77

maker, whether he lived millennia ago or in the century of Darwin, Marx and Freud, can solve an antinomy. These antinomies, says Kant, 'awakened me from dogmatic sleep'. As a scientist Freud slept this dogmatic sleep all his life.

With his shallow positivism – religion to be superseded by science – Freud is not different from Comte. Yet he is different from him. In Freud's work, though never in the works of Comte, we find profound insights about religion. We find them only if we read Freud critically. He is often Balaam, the prophet who without wanting it had to pronounce words of blessing.

As a psycho-analyst Freud is the great physician, the great healer. He is also doing the job of tearing the mask from the face of man. As a psychologist of religion – but only if properly read – Freud discovers important differences between Judaism and Christianity. Involuntarily, he often speaks on behalf of Judaism. In a discussion at the School of Psychiatry in Washington in 1957, (Martin Buber: *Nachlese* Heidelberg, 1965) Buber, dealing with Freud, called him a 'simplifier'. Buber represents all those who are themselves accomplices of Freud's simplifications. It is true that on the surface Freud's writings on religion repeat the prejudices and mistakes of Enlightenment and Positivism. A critical reader can ignore them. When this is done, the Freud who has gained profound insights into religion will be discovered. Jew and Christian alike can only bypass them to their own grave loss.

MOSES AND MONOTHEISM

In Freud's last publication *Moses and Monotheism,* it is again our task to understand Freud better than he understood himself. W. F. Albright in his *From the Stone Age to Christianity* writes: 'As a counterpoise to these serious, though exaggerated, theories we may be pardoned for saying a word about a futile but widely read example of psychological determinism – Freud's *Moses and Monotheism* (1939). This book is simply the latest of a long train of books and papers on history and religion which have been issued by Freud himself and other members of the psycho-analytical school during the past generation. Like them his new book is totally devoid of serious historical method and deals with historical data even more cavalierly than with the data of introspective and experimental psychology' (Baltimore, The Johns Hopkins Press 1946 pp. 74–75). Freud anticipated such criticism and answered it beforehand in his book: 'But we venture to be independent of the historians in other respects and to blaze our own trail' (p. 60). Against all the evidence Freud states 1) that Moses was an Egyptian, 2) that Moses was killed by his own people, 3) that Mosaic monotheism is the monotheism of the Pharaoh Ikhnaton.

It is obvious that many will be annoyed by Freud's treatment of the Bible. The truth is that 'it is one of the enigmas of history that the Hebrews were so little affected by the religion of Egypt, when both history and religion show such intimate contacts between the two' (T. J. Meek, *Hebrew Origins,* New York, Harper 1950, p. 143). Freud could have cured himself of his sympathies for Ikhnaton by reading any history book about Tommaso Campanella (died 1639 in Paris) who worked as pamphleteer and agitator in the cause of the Counter-Reformation. This Jesuit advocated a totalitarian state with the Pope as Sun-god regulating every detail of the citizens' lives in the fashion of Orwell's *1984.* The tradition of the totalitarian Sun-god-kingdom which Ikhnaton established is also found in the theology of the Incas. The sun sees everything, touches everything, watches everything. In the investiture struggle between Pope and Emperor the issue is which of the two should have the sacred sun-attribute. Here we must mention Louis XIV, the *roi soleil,* and, also of course, the contemporary scene which Freud saw around him: the ascendency of fascism and Nazism. Freud misunderstood Ikhnaton's Egypt, ruled by a *summa idea,* by one single political principle, as an empire founded on monotheism. The old man – he was eighty when he finished the last chapter of *Moses and Monotheism* – was unable to withstand what people around him had accepted as the dominant philosophy of the day: totalitarianism.

Obviously Freud, the great genius, the discoverer of the cosmos of the unconscious, is an amateur in the field of history. His amateurish handling of the historical facts is exasperating. Anybody could be forgiven for judging the value of Freud's *Moses and Monotheism* in not so polite terms. Those to whom the Bible means the most precious document in the possession of mankind must be shocked by Freud. But those people in particular who take an interest in the meaning of the Old and the New Testament should not be too quick in dismissing Freud's findings entirely. Freud has something important to say to both Jew and Christian. The fact that he says it despite himself makes his contribution all the more convincing.

Freud says – without any intention to do so – that Moses is a prophet. He says so by alleging that Moses is not a Jew but an 'Egyptian'. As a prophet Moses would not be like the majority of Jews, he would be different from them. The prophet is different from his own people. This might be the subconscious argument for Freud's making Moses an Egyptian. Another analysis is also possible. Moses is not a Jew, but an 'Egyptian', because the 'Egyptian' is for Freud the gentile, rooted in history and creative in history. The Jew, even standing and acting in history, remains rooted in creation. The Jew lives in history as the creature of God. Freud opposes the view that monotheism is a Jewish crea-

tion. Indeed, it is not. It is not any man's creation. Moses is
not like Mohammed the founder of a new religion. This is
said by Freud with the vision of his subconscious mind,
and we can accept it. The Creator of heaven and earth and
nobody else created monotheism. We agree with Freud that
no Jew could have created monotheism. But the premises
leading to Freud's 'no Jew' also lead to the conclusion 'no
Egyptian.'

With all this I think I have gone as far as is possible
towards understanding Freud's absurd thesis 'Moses – an
Egyptian'. It seems to me the only way to defend Freud
from making a literary contribution to the collaboration with
totalitarianism in his *Moses and Monotheism*. Austrians,
and Austrian Jews, too, for a time looked hopefully to
Mussolini. They saw his as one who might save them from
Hitler.

No analytical explanation, however, is necessary for the
allegation that Moses was killed by his people. In this case
Freud offers no original observation of his subconscious experience but gives a pedantic repetition of his thesis that
history begins with the slaying of the primeval father. As
psychologist Freud has observed this fact – and the word 'observed' must be stressed – in what he called 'primitive history'
and also in the history of the Christian gentiles. His discovery of this fact in Jewish history, too, – Moses killed by
his people – was not based on observation. He assumed that
what applies to Christianity must also apply to Judaism. The
'pious', according to Freud's theory, were always both Jews
and Christians. Freud's theories about matters concerning
religion are always worthless and erroneous. What has worth
for the Jewish and the Christian theologian is what springs
from the subrational well of his Jewish being.

Freud establishes that Judaism is a father religion.
Directly he does not say anything of the kind. But his 'vision'
shows him what was in the 'beginning'. In the 'beginning'
was a father. This is his Jewish message, told in an archaic
form, in the myth of the 'male leader of the horde', invented

81

by him. The myth is invented, made up. The root of the myth, deep down in the subconscious portion of his mind, formed by his forefathers, is not made up, is not invented, not created by man. It is real and therefore conveys unadulterated truth. 'In the beginning' was a father; the father represents eternal order. Later 'sons' took over and 'history' took place. In his own way the psycho-analyst Freud talks about the difference between Creation and history, between the Book of Genesis and the Book of Exodus. Unintentionally the psycho-analyst says: 'The Bible is true.'

Freud establishes that history begins with a guilt, with the patricide of the sons, which he describes in his own peculiar way, rejected by anthropologists as a fanciful story. The anthropologists are right. But Freud is right, too. As a persecuted Jew looking not benignly at Christianity, Freud discovered an essential characteristic of the Christian faith. Christian faith begins with a guilt which has to be atoned for. As a Jew, Freud rejects such an attitude. His rejection has nothing to do with his agnosticism. He may suppose it has. It has to do with the Jewish past, the past of many generations which have formed him. It has to do with the jubilant cry of Genesis i, 1 that the beginning is through God and is 'renewed every evening and morning', that there is a beginning without guilt, a beginning to which man can always return and live a new life. The Creation of heaven and earth happened only yesterday.

Freud establishes that monotheism begins outside history but says so by stating that it starts outside Jewish history. He says that it is a product of Egypt. Egypt, not the Jewish tribes represent the might, the refinement and the intellectuality characteristic of history. Again Freud is right. Monotheism was, as many scholars found out, also in the possession of primitive groups living on a pre-historic level. The historical process makes civilised man polytheistic through the variety of its aims. But Freud also establishes – again indirectly – that monotheism is the very centre of Judaism.

Freud pleads for monotheism like a nineteenth-century Maimonides. But whereas the Maimonides of the past could emancipate himself from Aristotle's highest idea, Freud could not emancipate himself from Haeckel's *scientism* in which one idea from the pantheon of human ideas, scientific truth, was regarded as the highest idea, and made the basis of a monism misunderstood as monotheism.

Yet Freud can rightly be compared with Maimonides and can be seen as involved in the prophetic struggle against the gods. Any atheist will approve of the development from the many gods to the one god and eventually to no god. Freud is not an atheist of this type. For the Jew the gods are real, and the One God more real. The names of the gods change, the plurality remains. The plurality of today consists of culture and civilisation, of nation and race, of art, science, economy and class. With his indictment 'illusion' Freud is more radically against the history of the day than Marx with his indictment 'superstructure'. The Jewish prayer-book puts into the mouth of the Jew the question 'Who is like unto Thee, O Lord, among the gods?' (Exodus xv, 11). Human creations, seen from the viewpoint of God's eternal Creation, provoke contempt of the prophets. There is something of this prophetic contempt in Freud's writings about religion and civilisation. Freud, living in a decadent age and affected by it, is still a great Jew, a Jew of prophetic stature.

Moses and Monotheism, Parts I and II, was published in German in 1937. It was at that time that Buber wrote his most profound essays defending Judaism against Nazi scholars who attacked it. He and Leo Baeck went from one Jewish congregation in Germany to another to lecture about Judaism, upholding it as it has to be upheld by Jews. German rabbis preached about the truth of Judaism from their pulpits in the dangerous presence of Gestapo officials who sent over-courageous preachers to concentration camps. Freud rewrote Part III of *Moses and Monotheism* in London. He used outdated material by nineteenth-century antisemitic Old Testament scholars. His book cannot be called anything but an attack on Judaism as Jews had taught it for two thousand years. How can we defend Freud from making a contribution to the anti-Jewish Nazi literature? Such an outrage was not his intention. He had the stubbornness of the genius who wanted to round off his various essays about religion with his view of Moses. A genius is not necessarily human in his creative urge. Freud is a genius who added to the somehow still medieval tripos – philosophy, ethics, aesthetics – a new outlook: psychology. After Freud psychology is more than the description of the human self. Psychological phenomena are acknowledged as capable of comprehending the reality surrounding man.

As a genius Freud is to be admired, in his humanity he is – with his 'Moses' – a failure. In the time of the most cruel persecution which his people had to endure, he wrote about Judaism without love, without understanding, without thinking of the consequences. An attempt to defend Freud should however be considered. There is in the biblical narrative the story of the little Moses in the bulrushes. World literature knows of similar stories showing the childhood of the later hero and genius in his aloofness from father and mother and family. Freud must have been attracted by this story about the childhood of Moses. He himself was a fatherless Jew, a person representing a fatherless generation. The genius is the fatherless man who is like Prometheus committed to his creative work without any consideration of God and man. Freud was a 'first generation' Jew to use the term coined in Anglo-Jewry and applied to Jews who are the first of their family to take the step from Eastern European, in fact medieval culture to the new Western world. In his new world the 'first generation' Jew is without the guidance and help of his family. He is alone, like Moses in the bulrushes. He is alone in a non-Jewish world and becomes a non-Jew, an Egyptian', as it seemed to Freud. Freud, the fatherless Jew, could regard 'our Father in heaven' only as a myth. That a myth can contain truth, Freud was not able to see.

Part Three

FATHERS AND SONS

HEROES AND MARTYRS

Hermann Cohen, the predecessor of Franz Rosenzweig in the history of modern Jewish philosophy, once explained his ethical humanism to a pious Jewish layman. When he had finished, the layman asked one single question: 'Where is the *boré olam* (the Creator of the world) in your philosophy?' Cohen answered: 'I am afraid, the *boré olam* has no place in my philosophy of ethical humanism.' In his old age, however, he revised this opinion.

Rosenzweig radically changed the situation. He brought the concept of Creation back into modern Jewish philosophy. The jubilant cry: 'In the beginning God created heaven and earth' is a statement which science cannot afford to ignore. We do not only have science as a source of information. We have information which is not scientific knowledge and yet communicates truth. The two benedictions over bread and wine are the first which the Jewish child learns to say. They praise the Creator of the world. Bread and wine are natural produce transformed by man into a refined gift of the earth. Both bread and wine show how Creation penetrates civilisation. With the two benedictions over bread and wine the Jew praises the possibility that the history of man can be a continuation of Creation.

A line in Chesterton's poem 'The White Horse' reads: 'The end of the world was long ago.' It was two millennia ago, at the first Christmas, when, according to the Christian faith, eternity entered time, and this event at that point in history changed all subsequent history: it redeemed every subsequent history. The Jew says, the Creation of the world happened today, because, as the *Yotser*, the morning prayer, announces, God renews his creation every day. Redemption for the Jew means history returning to the perfection of Creation. In Christianity redemption is a historical event, and since that event all subsequent history has to be raised to the glory of that first Christmas, of that

87

single event to understand which as the event of redemption is the content of revelation. In Judaism – Creation offering revelation; in Christianity – a point in past history continuously proclaiming revelation: this is the difference between the two faiths.

There is no biblical word for 'revelation'. When a Hellenistic Jew translated the Pentateuch into the Aramaic of the *Targum Onkelos,* he found the text of Exodus xix, 20 and of Genesis xi, 5 'And God came down' too anthropomorphic. He therefore translated it 'God revealed himself'. This is the moment, a moment in the history of Hellenistic Jewry, when the word 'revelation' entered the vocabulary of mankind. The prophets did not have a general concept of separate revelation. We may say that in the Hebrew Bible Creation offers revelation, and God is worshipped above all as Creator. In the New Testament God is worshipped above all as Redeemer. Not creation in the past, but redemption in the past provides revelation in the New Testament. The distinction between God the Creator on the one hand, and God the Redeemer on the other begins with the Gospels. They introduce two distinctions which are not found in the Old Testament: firstly the distinction between God the Father and God the Son, secondly that between creation and second creation. The second creation raises man into the realm of the spirit. The Greek dichotomy 'mind – body' has found its Christian equivalent 'spiritual – secular'. Karl Marx, rejecting any superstructure in history and Sigmund Freud, seeing the rational side of man rooted in the irrational depth of the subconscious are Jews. They therefore reject the Christian distinction between spiritual and secular. Jew and Christian differ in their approach to history.

'The Year One, on the other hand, the year of the Christian revelation, is a historical date. History therefore remains for the Christian the place where the door leading to eternity is to be found. Shakespeare speaks of Saint Crispin's Day as an event to be celebrated eternally, again and again. Henry V addresses his soldiers before the battle with these words:

> *'This story shall the good man teach his son;*
> *And Crispin Crispian shall ne'er go by,*
> *From this day to the ending of the world,*
> *But we in it shall be remembered –*
> *We few, we happy few, we band of brothers;*
> *For he today that sheds his blood with me*
> *Shall be my brother; be he ne'er so vile*
> *This day shall gentle his condition . . .'*

Here, on the eve of the fierce battle in which many will die with the battle cry 'God for Harry, England, and Saint George!', Shakespeare enumerates the doctrines of the Christian. 'Band of brothers' refers to Christian brotherhood. Brotherhood is and remains a Christian concept. Brotherhood replaces family bonds through an order not present in the created order. It refers to a new creation, called in Christian terminology: 'second creation'. The Church and Christian civilisation form the second creation.

'We few, we happy few' refers to Christian election. God chooses. To be chosen by God means for man to have no choice. In Christian election however, creative man has an active role to play. He transcends his human status in tragic, heroic self-chosen activity. This activity improves the human status, ennobles the status of the creature of God. This improvement on man, the creature, is his rise to the spiritual level. As Shakespeare puts it, man may be 'vile'. 'This day will gentle his condition.' This day is a day of battle and of the sacrificial death which always constitutes Christian faith. Many a soldier will die. Though, a thousand years may pass, people will still say, 'This was their finest hour,' or as Shakespeare puts it: 'From this day to the ending of the world . . . we in it shall be remembered.' Golgotha repeats itself in the Christian approach to history. Something repeats itself in this rise from the contemptible secular to the glorious spiritual level: Sacrificial death. Somebody must die that others may receive blessing. This is the Christian message. This message also says, somebody dies because he is killed: the noble soldier by his enemy, the crucified by his crucifier.

The Gospels, severed from the Old Testament by Marcion, see humanity as divided into two camps, the one differing from the other, as light is different from darkness. Together with the figure of Christ Antichrist enters the historic scene in the Marcionite heresy. According to Marcion the Old Testament is a book of the devil; the Jew is Antichrist. This is not accepted by orthodox Christian theology which recognises the continuing role of the Jew in Christian civilisation and thus evades the Marcionite heresy. Christians need the Jews. In their difference from the Jews Christians can explain their status as Christians. And yet, severing all links with the Jews they cease to be Christians and become merely gentiles.

Where Christianity is not deeply rooted in Judaism, it becomes Marcionite Christianity. This heretical Christianity concentrates exclusively on the second creation, on the spiritual superstructure above the created world. The historical scene develops into two opposing camps. The opposition spiritual – secular becomes an apocalyptic struggle between good and evil. A devil must be overthrown.

Jew and Christian are committed to history. But in each case the commitment is different. The Jew stands in history as the creature of God, as the whole man. After the first *churban,* after the first destruction of the Temple of Jerusalem, the Jewish people approached the prophet Ezekiel with a radical proposition. They suggested building a temple in Babylon. Their argument was: We are without a country of our own and without a state of our own. History has cast us out from the community of nations. Their suggestion: 'Let us build another temple' meant: 'Let us become a Jewish Church: let us become a religious organisation.' What they meant becomes clear from Ezekiel's answer. He said No, and said it in these words: 'And I passed by thee, and I saw thee weltering in thy blood, and I said unto thee:

"In thy blood live!" Yea, I said unto thee : "In thy blood live!" ' (xvi, 6). The Jewish people was after the first *churban* a people without a state and without a country and therefore different from the gentiles. Yet it was told by its prophet to live in history as do the gentiles. The commandment: 'Live in thy blood!' means: live as creatures of God, live as the Jewish people, do not live the spiritual life in which man the creator cuts himself off from Creation, live as a people, but live as the people of God. It was different at the second *churban*. After the dissolution of the Maccabean State a part of the Jewish people, the first Christians, stopped living as a people and began to live as members of a Church. Spirit, not blood, spirit, a turning away from the human situation, spirit, a leap of man, the creature, into a super-human situation, makes the Christian.

Changes in history are made by sons who revolt against their fathers. The Old Testament repeats again and again the phrase 'from generation to generation'. Abraham leaves his father's house and becomes a stranger in a foreign land. He does not revolt against his father. The *Midrash* which tells the story of young Abraham smashing the idols of his father is of late date. In the New Testament the phrase 'unto your children's children' does not occur a single time. The Christian Church begins as a revolt of sons against their fathers. Since this beginning Christians have a choice between two attitudes to the Jews: to love them as their begetters or to hate them as those whom the Church has to fight so that the spirit should prevail over the blood, the Church, the second creation, over Creation. The Christian Church, no longer aware of her roots in Judaism, will see the Jew as Antichrist and speak of the crucifixion as the murder of the son. Patricide, the murder of the father, is excluded as a possible commentary on what had happened. During World War I Richard Aldington expressed in his poem 'The Blood of the Young Men' the feeling which was central to the other war poets, especially Owen and Sassoon, that young men are sacrificed in large numbers for the good of those at home:

> *'Old men, you will grow stronger and healthier*
> *With broad red cheeks and clear hard eyes –*
> *Are not your meat and drink the choicest?*
> *Blood of the young, dear flesh of the young men.'*

The man on the Cross is a young man. 'The old Jew makes manifest in the look of his eyes and in the features of his face what is Jewish. It is, on the other hand, the type of a youth which makes visible what is characteristic for the Christian nations' writes Franz Rosenzweig (*Stern, III,* 191) who sees Christianity as an 'eternal youth movement'.

In the West, Christianity was at the time of its rise in fierce competition with the cult of Mithras, so popular with the Roman soldiers. Christianity won through its message, 'Somebody must die that others may live.' It prevailed against the cult of Mithras through its appeal to the Roman soldiers who fought the endless wars of the Roman Empire. The Roman sculptor of 'The Dying Gaul' bestows a bliss on the dying soldier which is spiritual and divested of all heroic self-assertion. Eventually the West created in the tomb of the Unknown Warrior a modern equivalent to the Cross on which the crucified body of a young man represents all the sons who die their sacrificial death on the battlefield.

A. J. P. Taylor writes in *English History, 1914–1945* 'England has ceased to be, in any real sense, a Christian nation' (pp. 259, 317, 319). It would be better to say of the time which he describes: everywhere the Christian Church had become Marcionite, disclaiming all responsibility for the process of history. The soldiers of the modern civilian armies suffered and were in their sacrificial death the only Christians in a world of pagan cruelty. 'Positive, aggressive heroism of the epic character is seldom possible in modern war; a man may perform valiantly in action, but for every valiant moment there are weeks of inactivity, boredom, suffering, and fear. Thus the virtues of the modern infantryman are Christian virtues – patience, endurance, hope, love –

rather than the naturalistic virtues of the epic hero' (J. H. Johnston about David Jones, quoted by Bernard Bergonzi in *Heroes Twilight,* Constable London, p. 210). A. J. P. Taylor is therefore wrong in his statement. He is proved wrong on every Armistice Day when the Last Post is sounded and the whole nation unites in silent devotion with those who pay their homage at the tomb of the Unknown Warrior. In this silence the Christian tenet of the Resurrection gives hope to those who have lost their dear ones in the battles of two world wars. The Jew has the promise of his prophet: 'He maketh death to vanish in life eternal; And the Lord will wipe away the tears from off all faces: And the shame of His people will He remove from off all the earth . . . '(Isaiah xxv, 8).

The second *churban* was Rome's destruction of Jerusalem, which led to the separation of Christianity from Judaism. The same separation took place during the holocaust of 1933–1945, now called the third *churban*. During these terrible years a Marcionite Christianity without connection with Judaism looked on while an antisemitism resembling nothing in history eventually culminated in the father-murder of Auschwitz. When Christianity withdraws into the realm of the spirit and disobeys or does not even understand Ezekiel's commandment 'In thy blood live', man, the creature of God, is abandoned, his blood is shed in the Christian cruelty which leaves history and does not interfere in the dominion of the gentiles.

Auschwitz happened in Christendom. Auschwitz is the Christian scandal. Auschwitz is the third *churban* which the Jewish people suffered for the sake of mankind. Auschwitz is a commentary on the second *churban,* which led to the separation of Christianity from Judaism. Auschwitz proves that Golgotha is partly patricide. The Cross should show a murdered father, not a murdered son. A father was killed by his son. The Jew is the father, the Christian the son.

The Jewish-Christian dialogue which is now in progress

93

is, indeed, an epoch making event. But this dialogue is idle talk if Auschwitz is excluded as a subject of the dialogue. Who is responsible for Auschwitz? The Germans of course. But this answer will not satisfy an Asian who disregards the national varieties within Europe and sees Europe as the Christian realm different from the Buddhist unity of Asia. 'Surely', an Asian intellectual said to a missionary, 'Hitler was a Christian.' To explain to him that Hitler was a secularised Christian, a heathen, will not satisfy the Asian observer of European affairs. Only in Christian lands is the secular opposed to the spiritual. Only there exists the unremitting tension between gentile and Christian. Only there can secularised Christians in their passion for a 'second creation' become guilty of a demoniac destruction of the creation, only there, but not in the lands of the Buddha. It was in a Christian country, not in the lands of the Buddha, that Hitler and those who followed him were born and bred.

The Church, established in history, the visible Church, as the Christians call her, is a secular institution. All secular institutions carry with them the mark of original sin. Secular history never has the innocence which is the glory of men, beasts and things in the world created by God. The Jew is in history as man created by God. The history of how man, the image of God, became man, cannot be recorded. He is there, as the miracle of the existence of the world is there, daily with us, but always transcending our understanding and only fittingly described in the liturgical praise of the Psalmist. Whereas the Jew is within history as the world created by God is within history, the Church is a product of history. As a product of history it carried the burden of original sin. The original sin of the Christian Church is her separation from Judaism. Centuries after the event to which the Gospels refer, the separation was prevented from becoming what it is in the Gospels of Marcion: an antisemitic Church, rejecting the Old Testament and hating the Jews. But Auschwitz proved that the original sin of the historical Church can re-create the conditions which once led to the Marcionite separation of Christianity from Judaism.

Antisemitism is of Christian origin. Not merely sociology and pathology, but also theology has to deal with antisemitism. We know next to nothing about the historical details of the first separation of Christianity from Judaism. But we do know the history of the Christian Church, and we also know what happened in Auschwitz. Those who had once received the word of God from the Jews deserted the Jews. The two-thousand-year-old Jew-hatred led to modern antisemitism and eventually to Auschwitz. In the beginning of Christianity Jewish sons tore themselves away from their Jewish fathers. When sons rebel against their fathers, the terrible sin of patricide looms over the divided family. Auschwitz was patricide. The guilt of the beginning of Christianity repeated itself at Auschwitz. Christian sons revolted against their Jewish fathers. Patricide was again committed. Auschwitz is the monument of a *judenrein* Christianity, of a de-judaised Christianity.

The historian is unable to observe the moment at which what is new rises in history. He can only record the events before and after this moment. This concerns Judaism more than Christianity. Judaism, the first monotheistic religion, appears in history like the miracle of the starry firmament, arising out of the darkness and shining in mighty splendour. Christianity participates to a smaller degree in this miracle. We see the chapters of Jewish Christianity and of gentile Christianity preparing the entry of the Christian Church. But her real beginning lies in the darkness where no historian can recognise any contours and where the Christian believer is thrown back to his faith which alone can tell him what happened. What happened? A schism? Judah Hallevi rejects this suggestion. He has the parable of the seed and the tree, Judaism being the seed, and Christianity being the tree which grows from this holy seed. Where the Christian Church does not accept the truth of this parable, she is thrown back to the time before she had rejected the Marcionite heresy. This heresy sees Jew and Christian as enemies.

The son who is an enemy of his father is a potential patricide. After the Middle Ages the dominant force on the stage of history is no longer a Church but a Christian world. The post-medieval Christian world gave birth to the Christian antisemite whom no Christian dogma tamed in his fury. This makes the guilt of the post-medieval Church even greater than that of the medieval Church, which was great enough. The patricide of Auschwitz throws light on the beginning of Christianity when its separation from Judaism took place. What happened then? We know now: sons rose against their fathers; patricide took place.

It has been said of Franz Kafka that he described in his novels the appalling situation of concentration camps long before the soil of Europe was fouled with the Nazi examples of them. Something similar can be said of Freud. He came face to face with the sin of patricide which the Church as Marcionite Church always commits. The post-medieval modern Church had become a Marcionite Church, a Church entirely cut off from Judaism and therefore no longer the 'tree' grown from the 'holy seed'. The Church is responsible for Auschwitz. The Nazis found a de-judaised Christianity on the scene and only drew a radical conclusion from what already existed. Freud sensed this situation and spoke of it. He did it in his way, as a child of his times, as a believer in science holding all the organised religions around him in contempt.

Relying on Robertson Smith's *The Religion of the Semites* Freud explained the origin of civilisation as a revolt of sons against 'the old male leader of the horde'. All the world told Freud that Robertson Smith's facts were unproved. Freud would not budge. What he could not defend as scientific fact, he called his 'intuition', and he never gave up what his intuition had conveyed to him. The way in which Freud was wrong is obvious but negligible. What is important is the way in which Freud was right.

Freud, like Franz Rosenzweig and Kafka, saw history around him as history motivated by Christian thought and,

therefore, as continuous war and revolution as the continuous revolt of sons against fathers. Freud, 'a master of the
written word', as the Swiss professor of literature Walter
Muschg calls him, used the word 'horde' for the group at
the beginning of history. He did not use the word 'herd',
which would place this group in pre-history. He used the
word 'horde' for the group which used violence as means of
action.

History as the history of states begins with an act of
violence. The state dispenses justice. But before it is in a
position to do so, it has to establish itself and this is done
with the help of violence. Justice and power are the two
pillars of the state. Every state begins with an act of over-
throwing a predecessor. The Greek cities invented myths to
hide this gruesome beginning. Christianity did away with
them but did justice to the memory of a guilt by teaching
the doctrine of original sin as characteristic of all gentiles
who as founders of cities and states become creative in
history. The guilt of the gentiles in politics is also incurred
by the makers of culture. Every artist becoming a creator
commits the sin of aspiring as man to be what God is, creator.
He neglects the ways and duties of the creature of God.
'The true artist will let his wife starve, his children go bare-
foot, his mother drudge for his living, sooner than work at
anything but his art' (G. B. Shaw).

Any Jewish preacher speaking about 'Jewish warmth'
will find his congregation in full agreement with him. On
the other hand, Kafka speaks about 'Christian coldness'.
Graham Greene in his novel *The Power and the Glory* shows
Mexico under communism, when Roman Catholic clergy
were forced to marry to evade persecution. One such priest,
having found his way back into the Church, meets his child,
now with a Roman Catholic priest as father, a fatherless
child. Graham Greene shows the whole tragedy of the situation. 'Why have I not got a father like the other children,'
the little one says. The priest is deeply moved but can do
nothing. A world cuts him off from his own flesh and blood.

It is the spiritual world to which he belongs as a Christian priest. A father in spirit cannot allow himself to be a father in the flesh – an example of the Christian coldness produced by the rise from the secular to the spiritual. He who follows Christ must leave father and mother, brother and sister.

Freud discovered the whole man. He rejected the Platonic dichotomy between mind and body and the Christian dichotomy spiritual – secular, and saw man, even in his highest flights of thought and imagination, rooted in the subconscious depth of the Creation. In this Freud is a great Jew. His theory of the male leader of the horde killed by his sons reflects history motivated by Christian teaching. The division spiritual – secular is, from the point of view of the 'mothers', seen as a cold denial of human happiness. And every son revolting against his father will say 'one has to love God more than one's father' and will by that justify the patricide of Christian history. What Freud thought to be the explanation of primitive history is in fact the explanation of Christian history. Freud, absolutely unversed in theology, is all the more convincing as his theory is based on observation. He observed the whole man, man rooted in the creation. He also observed contemporary history with clinical exactitude, and therefore discovered the patricide in Christian civilisation. 'The pious', as he termed them, were the Christians, and in antisemitic Vienna the Christians were his enemies. Kafka 'saw' a concentration camp before it existed, Freud 'saw' Auschwitz before the world knew the name of this place of patricide.

With his story of patricide of 'the murder of the male leader of the horde', Freud discovered a fact which he clearly observed but which he failed to understand. He discovered a guilt characteristic of a history under Christian influence. Where the Christian tension between spiritual and secular breaks up and leaves a secular history without spiritual influence, secular history begins with a guilt the consequence of which cannot be eradicated by future events. We know of three ways in which guilt can burden the conscience of man. Freud had discovered the guilt complex, the guilt as sickness of the mind. He made possible as a psycho-analyst a cure for this guilt complex, which he was the first physician to diagnose. The guilt complex is different from real guilt, from authentic guilt for which man is responsible before society and God. Besides the guilt complex and authentic guilt a third guilt exists which Freud also discovered and which he described in his story of patricide. The third guilt is 'built in' in history, and as original sin is recognised as such by Christian theology. It is the guilt of the first step which man makes when creative without God. Man, the creature of God assuming the role of his maker, burdens himself with guilt. This guilt becomes a burden like the guilt complex, and has its vengeance, like the authentic guilt, but is different from both. Original sin is the guilt in history where the Christian gentile interrupts the course of the created world by making a new beginning. How can man as creator avoid becoming a rebel against God who alone is Creator? This question means: how can original sin be avoided? This question is the Christian question, and Christianity offers the answer in its doctrine of redemption. It speaks of redemption, and redemption is more than for-giveness, it makes undone what has been done. Such redemp-tion, Christianity teaches, is achieved through the sacrifice of a ransom.

On the Jewish Day of Atonement the Jew says before God: 'I have sinned.' He does not say 'I am a sinner' in the way the Christian does. The Jew confesses 'I have sinned', and the Jewish liturgy answers with the word of God: 'I have forgiven.' On the Day of Atonement the Jew confesses his sins in all humility, he prays '*with* the sinners'. Although man has been created in possession of a 'pure soul', he is drawn into the contest of good and evil. Every man falls into the trap of sin. This does not make man a sinner who is a fallen angel through original sin. Christianity sees him as a sinner through no personal fault but through a creation to which the biblical attribute 'very good' would not be applicable. Tillich, in a Jewish-Christian dialogue said: 'I have met Jews who were very good people. But there is one fault which they all have: they have no sense of sin.' Indeed, Tillich should have said 'they do not understand the meaning of original sin'. Men who remain rooted in Creation, while active in history, do not understand why the resort to original sin is needed.

The Christian with his confession: 'I am a sinner' wants more than God's forgiveness. He wants God to change an existing situation. The Christian hope is redemption from a sin which he has committed without any chance of avoiding it, but which burdens every Christian: original sin. Every Christian is born a gentile and aspires through faith in the only Christian, Christ, to rise to a spiritual existence. No Christian regards himself as born a Christian. He can become one by leaving his gentile status behind, by becoming a 'new Adam', integrated into the 'second creation' and therefore freed from original sin. The statement 'the Jew is born a Jew' means: man born of woman can meet God. Creation is without the blemish of original sin.

An action can be forgiven, but the man who as creator has broken away from his status as creature of God, needs more than forgiveness. He needs redemption, that redemtion which the Gospels preach as their good tidings. It is a redemption achieved through a sacrifice. In the Old Testament Abraham offers Isaac as a sacrifice, but God holds Abraham back from slaughtering him. In the New Testament Isaac *is* sacrificed. The Christian interpretation of Genesis 22 is radically different from the Jewish reading of this chapter. The blood of the scapegoat redeems others from their sin, from the sin which cannot be forgiven and which needs redemption. The Christ of the Gospels is not the only scapegoat. Christ, the one scapegoat, stands for many scapegoats, for the hecatombs of sacrifices which history devours: soldiers, martyrs, Jews. Golgotha repeats itself on thousands of battlefields, in the permanent revolution of Christian history, in Auschwitz. The scapegoat is killed. Judaism, the faith of the prophets in which Abraham does not sacrifice Isaac, is a faith without a scapegoat. A Christianity not rooted in Judaism will see the death of a scapegoat, the death of soldiers, martyrs and Jews, in a spiritual light, and, in the context of the Gospels, as unavoidable. Jew and Christian preach good tidings for man's future. They proclaim the possibility of progress. But the Christian dogma sees progress as unavoidably connected with heroism and martyrdom in war and revolution. The Jew believes in a peaceful way of progress. *Pax* was the message to the fratricidal gentiles of the Roman Empire. *Shalom,* peace for mankind seen as a family, is a message to Jew, Christian and gentile.

After the second *churban,* the Christian calendar divides the ages into *ante* and *post Christum natum.* After the third *churban,* after Auschwitz, many Christians and Jews have already said 'the world is no longer what it was before'. Thus we have to distinguish between the worlds *ante* and *post* Auschwitz.

Herder, one of the leading German Romantics, said that each nation has its 'great hour' in history. The 'great hour' separates the past history of the nation from its subsequent history. With this allegation Herder transplants the order of Christian chronology into the history of the gentiles. In their own history, too, there is a 'great hour' like the one in which Christians divide world history into a period *ante Christum natum* and into one *post Christum natum.* In its 'great hour' a nation rises in creative power to the moment which is different from the ever-identical stream of human birth, life, and death and also different from the eternal cycle of the stars and the seasons. What happens in the 'great hour' is history; it is performed by masses of men, but the masses act as if they were not many but were a single actor. After the 'great hour' nothing is as it was before.

1914 was Europe's 'great hour': the flower of the manhood of the European nations went in selfless submission and in exalted spirit to the Golgotha of their battlefields. 1918 proved to be only an armistice, and when in 1945 the liberation arrived, the *churban* of Auschwitz, Treblinka, and Belsen became known to the world. Heroism and martyrdom were near to each other. To distinguish between them appeared to be wrong. In each case human beings had been sacrificed. Soldiers and Jews had been killed, they were – to speak in Christian language – crucified. In the language of Isaiah 53 the Christian gentiles can speak sentences which portray the Jewish inmate of the concentration camps:

> '... *as one from whom men hide their face:*
> *He was despised, and we esteemed him not.*
> *Surely our diseases he did bear, and our pains*
> *he carried; ...*'

1914 cannot be explained only by referring to nationalism, imperialism, patriotism, diplomatic short-sightedness and the lack of imagination on the part of the military. In the songs of the youngsters and in the sorrows of the adults there was a rise above everyday life, a readiness for sacrifice, and therefore there was something holy, something spiritual in those who marched away. Sacrifice is holy. Martyrs need not look, or be, as they were depicted by the less-gifted painters of the Middle Ages. Martyrs can be of the ordinary kind. A soldier is a soldier. He smokes his pipe, enjoys a drink and likes a joke. But the soldier's march to his 'great hour' often turns out to be his crucifixion. 1914 was the great hour which made an end to the world of the fathers. The sons died and in their deaths was the end of Europe's world of the fathers. The Middle Ages, still preserved in many pockets of resistance, collapsed in ruins. This is what happened in the years 1914–1945. The Eastern European bearded Jews represented the old European world of the fathers, destined to die. They died, but not in battle; they died by murder. The patricide concerned six millions.

We know very little about the exact moment in history when Christianity became separated from Judaism. Crucifixions often occurred in Roman Palestine and everywhere in the Roman Empire. But we do know the events of the years 1914–1945. The 'great hour' of those years was the rise of a revolution in the midst of which we still live. Sons went new ways. In all the capitals of Europe, in the villages and in the hamlets, the sons marched away in August 1914 and did so with an enthusiasm which is today difficult to understand, unless we remember what kind of heart the heart of the young is. It is full of love, but not that love which binds human being to human being. It is something else. It is love burning to render the greatest sacrifice. The sons marched away filled with sacrificial love. They marched towards an altar. They marched as crusaders determined to fight infidels and to conquer the holy city.

Golgotha, the story of the crucifixion, is not recorded in a way which allows us to sort out in neat detail: here is the father, here is the son. In the carnage of battle it is not like that either. The dead are fathers, and the dead are sons. But the Gospels seem to adopt a position which they assume to be accurate. On the Cross hangs a son. Why a son? Was it not the son who rebelled against the father? Was not the deicide in which a man with the image of God in himself was killed *patricide*? Should not the man on the Cross be a bearded patriarch of the kind which the Germans mocked, murdered and tortured in Poland? In the Orthodox Church ikons portray a bearded Christ who is no longer young. This is strange only to the western mind, but reminds us that father and son are one, and that the tragedy of the one is connected with the tragedy of the other.

The Tomb of the Unknown Warrior, this modern form of the symbol of the Cross, commemorates the dead of two world wars. When man is killed, deicide occurs. The Christian symbol of the God killed by man cannot but remind Christians of the Jews who perished, because Christians shouted 'Kill the Jews!' It is a Christian story which tells of people shouting their antisemitic 'Crucify him, crucify him!' This story repeated itself in Auschwitz and the other camps which the Germans built, as the Romans erected the Cross when they set out to kill.

APOCALYPSE AND *CHURBAN*

Christian terminology is employed when Auschwitz is now called an 'apocalyptic event'. The book of the New Testament called 'Revelation' belongs to the type of writing which is nowadays called underground literature. The enigmatic phraseology is necessitated by the impossibility of speaking freely in a time of persecution. To speak of the 'Apocalypse of Auschwitz' puts the early Christians living in an anti-Christian Roman period on the same level as the Jews under Nazi terror. 'The Four Horsemen of the Apocalypse' who were given 'power over a quarter of the earth, with the right to kill by sword and by famine, by pestilence and wild beasts' (vi, 8), did indeed ride through the world from the Atlantic coast of France up to North Africa and Southern Russia. Those who carried out these killings on a massive scale 'worshipped the beast also, and chanted "Who is like the Beast? Who can fight against it?" The beast was allowed to mouth bombast and blasphemy and was given the right to reign . . . 'It opened its mouth in blasphemy against God, reviling his name and his heavenly dwelling. It was also allowed to wage war on God's people . . .' (xiii, 4–7).

Apocalypse is the Greek word for revelation. John sees God on his throne, and near him 'the lamb'. The lamb, the animal sacrificed on the altars of Jerusalem, represents Christ in a Christian exegesis of a verse from the Servant of God texts: 'He is brought as a lamb to the slaughter' (Isaiah liii, 7). If the ashes of those buried in Auschwitz were not those of Jews, Christian sentiment would find it appropriate to erect a huge cross at Auschwitz as a fitting memorial. The catastrophe which the name Auschwitz conveys to our age and to subsequent ages could be commemorated in this

104

way by Christians. But it cannot be done. Auschwitz means six million Jewish martyrs, and Christians must stand in awe in the face of a martyrdom in which Jews, not Christians, were the main sufferers and in which Christians are forced to search their consciences and to ask whether they are not implicated in what happened.

The New Testament book 'The Revelation of St John' sees revelation in the framework of a catastrophe taking place in history. How do Jews, on the other hand, connect history with revelation? We have pointed out that according to the Hebrew Bible the creation of the world is the content of revelation. Christian doctrine, however, sees revelation taking place at a distinct point in history. This doctrine makes history all-important, to such a degree that the world, created by God, and God, the Creator can move into the background of Christian consciousness. The Redeemer is worshipped, the Creator forgotten. The Son is more important than the Father for Christian faith, especially for a faith uprooted from Judaism.

The whole Jewish people today must see itself as the survivors of Auschwitz. Everyone is today a survivor. Western man is a survivor of World Wars I and II. The survivors rub their eyes and are surprised to be alive. They ask: what happened? They ask: What is history? What does history convey to us? Must it convey something, or must it convey nothing? What is the condition under which history can convey something to man?

Moses Mendelssohn is usually seen as the first Jew who had entered the postmedieval chapter of the Jewish people. His statement 'history bores me'* can be taken as expressing the approach of the Enlightenment which saw past history, especially the Middle Ages, as a dark age, now, at last, moving forward into the age of reason. But Mendelssohn need not necessarily be understood in this way. Perhaps he is in

---

* See Cassirer: *Die Idee der Religion bei Lessing und Mendelssohn, Festgabe zum zehnjährigen Bestehen der Akademie für die Wissenschaft des Judentums, Akademie-Verlag*, Berlin, 1929, p. 32.

harmony with the Psalmist's attitude towards the gentiles: 'He that sitteth in heaven, laugheth, the Lord hath them in derision' (ii, 4). The Psalmist remains passionately interested in history and expresses his contempt, not of history, but of those who in history rebel against God.

> *'Why are the nations in uproar?*
> *And why do the peoples mutter in vain?*
> *The kings of the earth stand up,*
> *And the rulers take counsel together,*
> *Against the Lord, and against his anointed:*
> *Let us break their bonds asunder,*
> *And cast away their cords from us'*
>
> (ii, 1–3)

Mendelssohn's lack of interest in history represents the attitude of superiority which the European Jew in the Middle Ages displayed towards his surroundings. Outside his ghetto he did not see the 'Christian West', he only saw power politics, bloodshed, brutality and drunkenness.

The Romantic period led, especially in Germany, to the century of the great historians. Jews, too, turned to history and investigated their past. The Jewish historians regarded their work as capable of leading to a gentile rehabilitation of the Jewish people. As soon as the world realises the holiness of the Jewish past, it was said, the miserable state of the oppressed Jewish people will be seen as injustice and relieved by the civilised nations. The historians will achieve Jewish emancipation. What German Jews called *Wissenschaft des Judentums* was mostly the work of historians; *their* craft was *Wissenschaft* (science, learning). Splendid results were achieved in the century of the *Wissenschaft des Judentums*. One of its first results was Abraham Geiger's rehabilitation of the Pharisees which shed new light on the New Testament. Christian scholars took note of the findings of Jewish Learning, and Jewish and Christian Biblical and post-Biblical scholarship harvested its triumphs. Above all, the thought that history is a progressive process filled the

Jewish generations between Mendelssohn and 1914 with an optimism which was identified with the very faith of the prophets and the classical rabbis.

This optimism was shattered by the apocalyptic event of the Great War. When events are viewed as apocalyptic, the historian is no longer the person to deal with them. Consequently a critical approach to the historian made itself felt. He was accused of having become a mere chronicler of meaningless events. 'Tomorrow and tomorrow and tomorrow, a tale told by an idiot signifying nothing.' Nihilism crept into the hearts of those who had believed in the stability of the contemporary historical world. Death and nothingness stared into their faces, and death and nothingness became the problems of those thinkers who were called existentialists. What was common to them was despair. Sartre's nihilism is, above all, the hangover after the Nazi invasion of France. In these years of despair, frustration, humiliation and disgust Sartre's existentialism has its roots. Heidegger's existentialism had similar reasons. With him it was the defeat of Germany after 1918 which preceded the publication of his main work *Sein und Zeit* (Being and Time) in 1926. Six years earlier Franz Rosenzweig had written his *Stern der Erlösung*. He wrote the first notes of this work as a soldier at the front. Nevertheless his message was a message of hope and not of despair. The ways in which Franz Rosenzweig belongs to and remains apart from the philosophical school of existentialism have to be carefully considered.

All the existentialist thinkers from Pascal and Kierkegaard to Heidegger, Rosenzweig excluded, are 'philosophers of despair'. Pascal is the first to feel deeply the loss of the belief in a created world and its replacement by the Newton-Cartesian 'nature'. He speaks of 'this remote corner of nature' in which man 'should regard himself as lost', he speaks of 'the little prison cell in which man finds himself lodged, I mean the (visible) universe' (*Pensées*, ed. Brunschvig, p. 72). But still, Pascal remains faithful to the 'God of Abraham, Isaac and Jacob'. Kierkegaard does not end up in nihilism either. He remains a Christian. He even significantly criticises Hegel, in whose system historical necessity, understood as political necessity, had obliterated the uniqueness of man. But Pascal and Kierkegaard are not the teachers and fore-runners of Sartre. Sartre is like Heidegger, who is entirely a nihilist. In 1933 he addressed the students of Freiburg University as its Chancellor – not in his academic robes, but in S.-A.-uniform. When at that time he met his philosophical mentor of many years, Edmund Husserl, he passed the old Jewish sage by without a greeting. He may have later deplored the speech which he delivered in 1933, yet he stands in the history of philosophy as the German philosopher in S.-A.-uniform. His whole philosophical writings justify this picture as congenial to the philosopher of nihilism who severed all his links with the Christian faith.

Heidegger shares with the German romantics a constant reference to death. There is a romanticism in England, in France, and in Germany, but only in Germany is romanticism pre-occupied with death. No nation has pondered about death as much as the German. Clemenceau, who knew the Germans very well although he did not love them, said: 'In the soul of the Germans ... there is a lack of understanding of what life really is, of life's charm and greatness. How these people love death! One has only to read their poets: everywhere you find the reference to death.' Heidegger, the German existentialist, sees death in the centre of human existence; he defines life as 'running towards death'. How different is Franz Rosenzweig who writes: 'When death unmasks himself in your last hour, he will say to you: "Don't you know me, I am your brother?"!' Rosenzweig finishes his great work *Der Stern der Erlösung* with the words: 'Where does the way lead us? Don't you know? It leads into life', and according to his directions to the printers 'life' is to be written in capital letters: LIFE.

Fichte and Hegel led to Heidegger. These two German thinkers regarded themselves and were regarded as bringing the spirit of Greece to the German people. This was another

way under the prevailing circumstances of expressing the
fact that their philosophy cut itself off more and more from
Christian roots. In their search for revelation these thinkers
look exclusively to history, to man alone, to man without
God. In this they resemble the Gnostics of old. Gnosis
means knowledge. Revelation was thought possible as
knowledge. Gnosticism was the 'hellenisation of Christianity'
(Harnack) and post-Kantian German philosophy achieved a
hellenisation of the German people. Instead of 'hellenisation'
we can also say 'paganisation'. The so-called German philosophy of idealism was a philosophy of history which also,
like Gnosticism, looked exclusive to Promethean man as the
sole creator of history. Of him a knowledge was expected
which should include God and the universe. This was Gnosticism on German soil, this was the German heresy, born
in the studies of the German philosophers and leading to
Nietzsche's nihilism, proclaiming 'God is dead'. A God con-
structed by the philosophers is a 'dead God'. A God who
is only a God of history, the Redeemer of the Christian
Gnostic, and not also as Creator a God of the universe becomes a 'dead God'.

> *Who once has lost*
> *What thou has lost stands nowhere still*

said Nietzsche to modern man, whose universe was no longer
creation, but only 'nature', physical nature, and above all,
man-made history.

In the civilised West outside Germany the question 'Can
it happen here?' is often asked. It is more revealing to understand why it was bound to happen in Germany. The entire
post-Kantian philosophy lost its connection with the West,
with Hume and Locke, whom Kant had carefully studied.
Fichte, Schopenhauer, Hegel and Nietzsche are the leading
philosophers of what in Germany was called 'German idealism' and what in historical perspective is better called German 'Gnosticism'. Faust is the fatherless man, and he is the
German Prometheus who inspired the post-Kantian philo-

sophers. Faust, the Ego without family and fellow-man, becomes in Fichte's and Schopenhauer's solipsism the Atlas of Homeric mythology and the maker of history. Goethe's 'way to the mothers', his reverence of nature as the Great Mother, was a rebellion against the father. The rabbis of the Hellenistic age and the Church of that time recognised the danger of Gnosticism. Nobody, or too few, rejected German Gnosticism with its Marcionite anti-Jewishness. Hitler came. It was bound to happen. To understand the German heresy is more revealing than any answer to the question: 'Can it happen here?' can be.

Where history is emancipated from the world created by God and becomes a process without a transcendent realm beyond man, the door is open to nihilism. The philosophy of history of Fichte and Hegel was bound to lead to the nihilism of Heidegger. In a letter written on April 12th 1926, Goebbels defined nihilism as 'the courage to destroy, to crush those things which were once holy to us, such as tradition, education, friendship and human love'. Auschwitz is the monument of German nihilism. German university professors had educated German youth to see in the history of the German nation a self-sufficient 'absolute'. When this history faced its disaster in 1918, the believers in a holy German history were left with nothing. The way to nihilism was open.

The German post-Kantian idealistic philosophy generated that nihilism which eventually led to Auschwitz. The Germans were taught from school to the grave to seek edification entirely in history. Victories and battles, revolutionary and conservative enactments, in fact men alone, were seen as the creators of history. History was reduced to visible facts, and what invisibly moves history from outside, from a sphere transcending history, was not considered. Where man makes himself the Atlas of history, the breakdown is bound to follow. It did follow. Nietzsche with his 'God is dead' diagnosed merely the end-result of the German philosophy of history. When man looks only to history to find revelation and blasphemously calls the world a creation of the human

Ego, of man's *Erzeugung* (production), as did Fichte, when he sees the world as 'World as Will and Imagination' – the title of Schopenhauer's main work—, he encounters in history a non-Ego. A non-Ego created by mere abstraction, the *via negativa* of the materialist, is – a nothing. This nothing must be identified in one way or another and was eventually seen as something cruel, as Moloch. This was the way of German philosophy leading to Hitler and Goebbels. German philosophy was unable to halt the invasion of Germany by the Austrian Nazi ideology.

Fichte and Hegel still thought of themselves as 'Greeks'. They were Greeks not like Plato but like the Christian Gnostic Marcion. In speaking of an Absolute they still thought they were speaking of the demiurge of Greek philosophy. But they soon moved away from the demiurge of an ordered cosmos. A cosmos with an immanent logos was in Pharisaic Palestine associated with the Jewish teaching of a world created by God. But a philosophically-constructed Absolute is a *nihil*, it is in no respect a something. This Absolute may be thought of as a transcendent being, but it has lost the characteristic of that transcendence with which the God of the Hebrew Bible is associated. No *nomos* emanates from this philosophical transcendence, no law for the world and none for human action. To quote Heidegger's interpretation of Nietzsche: 'The phrase "God is dead" means that the supra-sensible world is without effective force' (*Holzwege* p. 200). Hans Jonas, the best expert in gnostic literature, confesses that Heidegger's philosophy was to him the key which unlocked the closed door which had barred for so long the way to an understanding of Gnosticism (*The Gnostic Religion*, Second Edition, Beacon Press, Boston). In antiquity Gnosticism rejected the testimony of the universe pointing to a benevolent creator. The Gospel of Marcion shows the gnostic contempt for a 'Jewish God', i.e. for a creator-God. 'Turning up their noses, the utterly shameless Marcionites take to tearing down the work of the Creator: "Indeed," they say, "a grand production, and worthy of its

111

God, is this world!" ' (Tertullian Contra Marc. I, 13).

German nihilism was radical nihilism, eventually different even from Gnosticism. German antisemitism is also different from Marcion's anti-Jewishness, from his rejection of the Old Testament. Marcion's Gnosticism was Christian heresy, but was still Christian. The German nihilism of the Nazis was a revolt against two thousand years of Christianity. German nihilism makes the German Siegfried more responsible for Auschwitz than the rest of the western world in the nineteenth century. The West to some degree also confessed a Christianity of the Marcionite pattern, forgetting the Creator as against the Redeemer and blind to the rightful place of the Jew in a Christian civilisation.

After the defeat of Hitler, Georges Bernanos wrote to Karl Barth the following remarkable letter: 'Nothing is left to us, I think, except to pray for Germany silently and from the depth of our soul. We must pray for Germany which, though defeated, has not yet arrived at the end of her destiny. Perhaps it is a wonderful sign of her destiny that she is given freedom, to suffer her terrible experience to the bitter end. May it please God to let Germany suffer, in her soul and in her flesh, according to the measure of her unlimited ability to suffer. May it please God that Germany repent entirely and abundantly, even beyond human strength. When she has paid for her guilt in the cry of her heart seeking expiation, may she also atone for our sins and gain expiation for the victorious nations who are not worthy to be her judges.' These wonderful words were written by a Frenchman to a Swiss at a time when Germany was in ruins. That seems long ago, today. Today Germany is the country of the economic miracle, and a new generation has grown up which wants to forget and to be acquitted from the verdict which the older generation had to accept. This new generation may say: 'The fathers have eaten sour grapes, why should the children's teeth be set on edge?' (Ezekiel xviii, 2).

Bernanos goes too far in speaking of 'the victorious nations unworthy of being Germany's judges'. Many speak now of the complicity of the Western nations in what happened to the Jews. 'America closed the doors against Jewish immigration on a large scale.' 'The West stood by inactively, when the worst was already known.' 'Why did the Allies not bomb the crematoria of Auschwitz?' (Arthur D. Morse: *While Six Million Died,* Secker & Warburg, London, 1968). Mankind is certainly an undivisible whole. So far the Western nations, as Bernanos implies and as the Germans now readily repeat, are implicated in the German guilt. There is some truth in this. The whole Christian West stands accused in the face of Auschwitz. But it should not be overlooked that the philosophy of nihilism had its stronghold in Germany and followed as a logical consequence from preceding German history. The deification of the state and the assumption of revelation within culture, within the various forms of art, was the German blasphemy.

Adolf Harnack (1851–1930), the renowned German Church-historian, himself a liberal and in his private life not an antisemite, displayed all the animosities of Marcion against the Old Testament. Like Marcion he praised the New Testament as the Gospel of Redemption and decried the value of the Old Testament. He made his choice of what he liked and what he disliked in the Old Testament – and he disliked certain essential parts of it.

In view of the close relationship between *The Apocalypse of John* and the gnostic book *The Gospel of Marcion* it appears quite appropriate for Christians today to speak of the 'apocalyptic event' of Auschwitz. In the *Apocalypse of John* 'apocalypse' means revelation, but revelation in which history reveals Moloch. Adolf Hitler, hailed by Germans as the Redeemer, turned out to be the Moloch, bringing death and destruction. A history in which man alone is the Promethean agent, a history in which man and not God who created heaven and earth is the Lord of history, leads to catastrophe. We Jews can therefore agree when Auschwitz is called an apocalyptic event, an event revealing Moloch in history. Man who does no longer understand himself as the creature of

H 113

God and as His beloved son, becomes the creator of a history in which the Moloch, devouring untold sacrifice, comes to the fore. The Moloch is a reality. He is man when he becomes a wolf to his fellow-man.

Primo Levi, a survivor of Auschwitz, describes in his book *If This is a Man* (The Orion Press Ltd., London) how the camp inmates were selected by an S.S. subaltern to be exterminated in the crematorium. It is decided in a second who goes to the right and who to the left. Everybody knows the left is the *schlechte Seite,* the bad side. Those who no longer seemed to be fit for hard work, were directed to the left. Let us hear the report of Primo Levi: '... from my bunk, on the top row, I see and hear old Kuhn praying aloud, with his beret on his head, swaying backwards and forwards violently. Kuhn is thanking God because he has not been chosen.

'Kuhn is out of his senses. Does he not see Beppo, the Greek in the bunk next to him, Beppo who is twenty years old and is going to the gas-chamber the day after tomorrow and knows it and lies there looking fixedly at the light without saying anything and without even thinking anymore? Can Kuhn fail to realize that next time it will be his turn? Does Kuhn not understand that what has happened today is an abomination, which no propitiatory prayer, no pardon, no expiation by the guilty, which nothing at all in the power of man can ever clean again?

'If I were God, I would spit at Kuhn's prayer' (p. 151).

The prayer which could passionately be prayed in Auschwitz was the outcry: 'My Lord, my Lord, why hast thou forsaken me?' (Ps. xxii, 2) No other prayer was possible for those who had been delivered into the hands of Moloch. Moloch was present in Auschwitz, he was a German in S.S.-uniform. And where was God? The Biblical prophets taught the Jewish people not to identify God with Moloch; the rabbis and the Christian doctors protested against the gnostic dualism which allowed Satan-Moloch a place in God's world. But in Nazi-Germany the Moloch was a reality. Hell, as the Middle Ages saw it, came to life in Auschwitz. Auschwitz was a man-made Hell. Man who wanted to create history without God, became a Moloch. The theological protest against the concept of a Moloch and against a belief in hell remains a valid defence of God. But this defence cannot refer to man, 'if this is a man' who can become a Moloch and can create hell.

It is time for the pinpricks and superficialities of the Christian apologist who speaks of the 'Moloch in Yahve' and censures him for demanding Abraham's son as sacrifice to stop. The death of the six million in Auschwitz, of the many more millions which the age of Auschwitz devoured in violence and cruelty, can be understood by the Christian as the price to be paid for the Christian doctrine of original sin, or as the sacrifice which has to be rendered in a history under the sign of the 'lamb', under the sign of the crucified 'son'. For the Jew every war is an unnecessary war, progress in history and faithfulness to God are possible without the sacrifice of Isaac. In a Christian understanding of history Isaac is sacrificed on the altar of God. In the Christian understanding any progress, including the progress from Hitler and Stalin towards an age which is once again human and rules by man's fear of God, inevitably involves the shedding of the martyr's blood.

True, the martyrs are dead. So far the Christian exegesis of Genesis 22, the Christian view of the encounter of Abraham with God, is correct. Jewish exegesis, on the other hand, sees this encounter as a trial. It is the temptation of Abraham. Abraham is 'tested'. Thus it says in the first verse of this chapter, which no man can ever read and remain calm. Breathless, and with his heart beating, any reader hears God saying: '... "Abraham"; and he said: "here am I." And He said: "Take now thy son, whom thou lovest, even Isaac, and get thee into the land of Moriah; and offer him there for a burnt-offering upon one of the mountains which I will tell thee of." ' (Genesis, xxii, 1, 2) The commandment 'Thou shalt love the Lord thy God with all thine

115

heart, and with all thy soul and with all thy might', and the commandment to Abraham, 'give me what is more precious to you than your own life', are one and the same. But what is really demanded from Abraham – and herein lies the difference between the Jewish and the Christian exegesis – is Abraham's *readiness* to offer the sacrifice; the sacrifice itself is not demanded – a fact which was not known beforehand. Abraham could only be truly tested when the sacrifice was demanded in absolute seriousness.

The Jewish martyrs of the third *churban* have gone. They have gone like the other millions sacrificed on the altar of the Nazi-Moloch. But after the third *churban* the surviving Jewish people is still on trial; every Jew is tested in his faithfulness to the God of his fathers. Auschwitz proved the utter political weakness of the Jewish people. Every Jew who remains a faithful Jew after Auschwitz is Abraham steadfast amid the uncertainty whether God will decide to accept or not to accept the sacrifice. After Auschwitz Jews who believe in God, the just and merciful pass the test in which they are tried today, as Abraham was tried before them. Jews must see the third *churban,* as their ancestors saw the first and the second *churban:* as a victory of God. *Churban* is not only the destruction of the old order, it is also progress into a new chapter of history. We, the Jewish people after Auschwitz, make this statement and proclaim the victory of God. In doing so we are in a state of mind which we often witness in the Psalmist: he cries out against his predicament and yet rejoices in the victory of God.

The first *churban,* the destruction of the Temple of Solomon – let us repeat the often-reiterated lesson of Jewish history! – made the Jewish people a people of the Diaspora. For the first time mankind had in its midst a people without a land and without a state and yet pursuing a mission in history, a holy mission. The second *churban,* the destruction of the Temple of Herod, signified the end of the Maccabean State and established the Synagogue in the Mediterranean world. For the first time mankind saw a form of worship in

116

which no blood was shed: prayers took the place of sacrifice; worship was constituted by the spoken word alone. The third *churban*, the *churban* of our time, also destroyed a holy Jerusalem: the religio-cultural unity of the Ashkenazi and Sephardi Diaspora in Europe and North Africa, the medieval unity created by the rabbinic interpretation of the Jewish Law. Destroyed is the medieval frame of the Jewish people, which after the third *churban* must either live as a westernised Jewry or disappear from the scene of history. What has been destroyed has lasted as long as the Roman Empire, which finally went down with the end of the Hapsburg, Hohenzollern, Tsarist and Ottoman empires. Their end and the end of rabbinic law have the same historical reason: the end of the Middle Ages. The interpretation of Jewish Law remained unchanged from the days of the *Mishnah* to the third *churban*. The medieval civilisation, Jewish, Christian, Islamic, is over. The Jewish Middle Ages lasted longest. After the third *churban* the attire woven in the Middle Ages is no longer appropriate for the Jewish people. Those of us who insist on wearing the kaftan and the Polish fur hat in the twentieth century are like those who nostalgically look back to the times when feudal lords prevented a sensible land reform and the liberation of the peasants in Eastern Europe. But the thousand-year-old tyranny of the Germans over the Slavs has come to an end. It began with the man-hunt of the Prussian Templars, who behaved as the S.S. did later and ended with the Oder-Neisse line. The Slavs are free. We Jews do not wish to remain 'Ashkenazim', medieval German Jews, or Sephardim, Jews of the Islamic cultural pattern. We look forward to our new duties as westernised Jews.

After these statements necessarily concerning only the past we look for a glimpse of hope into the future. This, but only this can be said, with certainty: after the third *churban* the Diaspora of the Jewish people will be a world-Diaspora. In Israel the expression 'the third *churban*' is not used. Instead, they use the word *'sho-a'*, which only means 'catastrophe' and is without any religious connotation. The Israelis feel that they are building up the third common-wealth in Israel. They are justified in so thinking. But the third commonwealth is not restricted to Israel alone. It is built everywhere by Jews in their world-diaspora.

To be hopeful or not to be hopeful after the third *churban* – this is the test by which the Jewish people are tried. After Auschwitz it would be natural for Jews to be full of despair. After Auschwitz it would be natural for the Jew to fail in the temptation in which Abraham was tried. We could even say: it would be human for the Jews after Auschwitz to stop being the people which brings the good tidings of the just and merciful God to mankind. By seeing the *churban* not only as an apocalyptic catastrophe, but as the awful (*nora* in Hebrew) work of God who leads mankind forward, we overcome despair and begin to hope. We ask: what kind of progress after the third *churban*? Where is the victory of God which can be celebrated today, as we celebrated one after the first and the second *churban*? We need not go into details. Hope if specified becomes calculation rather than hope. But we can specify the progress which will follow the third *churban* by saying: the Diaspora of the Jewish people, now a people of the post-medieval Western world, will be-come a world-diaspora.

Parallel to the widening of the Jewish Diaspora to a world-diaspora is the world-diaspora of Christianity. Asia has opened itself to the West, and Christianity will prove itself as the 'eternal youth movement', as the rising of the world of the sons against the world of the fathers. It will, as the eternal mission to the gentiles, convert the Buddhists and rejuvenate Asia.

When Jew and Christian speak to each other in peace, the world has peace. They are, of course, different from each other. We Jews see history realistically. We remember Auschwitz. History is not yet redeemed. With this view we differ from the Christian. The Jew worshipping in his family and testifying in the world to God as the Creator of the world,

118

and the Christian worshipping the Redeemer and rejoicing in the world, assumed as redeemed, are as different from each other as Jew and Gentile are different, and yet they are as near to each other as fathers and sons. It is in the peace prevailing between fathers and sons that the peace of the world grows.

A fatherless generation becomes a generation of cruel zealots, rejecting peace and choosing war. It hails a Messiah and forgets that within history every Messiah is a false Messiah. 'Historic revelation', i.e. belief turning to history alone, leads towards an apocalyptic situation: a man who believes in a utopia round the corner is crushed by history, and the many involved in such history perish. The Pharisees were aware that both Zealots and Essenes had misinterpreted the messianic faith of the Biblical prophets. The Dead Sea Scrolls show the closeness which existed between Essenes and Zealots. The Essenes were not Christians, but they were a sect developing towards Christianity.

The Cross is the symbol of final messianic redemption. It can also point to the apocalyptic disorder in which zealot sons rise against their fathers on their way through history. The Prophets warned the people: 'The Day of the Lord? It is darkness, not light' (Amos, v, 19). The Rabbis warned them, too: 'The Messiah? – I do not want to see him' (Talmud Sanhedrin 98). Freud warned our own generation: 'The new era is hastened in through patricide.' A Cross for Auschwitz? It would proclaim that what happened was patricide.

Both *churban* and Apocalypse express Jeremiah's terrifying words: 'For death is come up into our windows, It is entered into our palaces, To cut off the children from the street, And the young men from the broad places—' (ix, 20). But there is a difference, which prompted the Rabbis to exclude books inspired by apocalyptic vision from Holy Scripture. In the Apocalypse of John there is an impostor, a satan, and he is a false Messiah. This dualism is not overcome by the belief in a true Messiah. The true Messiah exorcises the false Messiah. With the Cross Christianity condemns all the Hitlers of history. This is the glory of Christianity. The choice between the true and the false Messiah remains. This is the predicament of Christianity. A Cross at Auschwitz would proclaim the victory over Hitler. But with the word *churban* the Jew looks only to God and to nobody else. The mourning Jew visiting Auschwitz as a pilgrim says *kaddish,* the prayer praising the Kingdom of God. In this prayer said by any Jew at any graveside he is alone with his God who is God alone. *Churban,* any catastrophe in history, does not contradict the oneness of God, does not curtail His justice and mercy. In the *churban* no reference to Satan is implied, the visionary of the Apocalypse does not cease to wrestle with him.

Mark xiii, 12, usually called the 'little Apocalypse' reads: 'Brother will betray brother to death, and the father his child; children will turn against their parents and send them to their death.' In the Talmud (Sanhedrin 97a) we find a similar saying: 'It has been taught: Rabbi Nehorai said: In the generation when the Messiah comes, young men will insult the old, and old men will stand before the young (to give them honour); daughters will rise up against their mothers, and daughters-in-law against their mothers-in-law. The people shall be dog-faced, and a son will not be abashed in his father's presence.' But Mark has his advice for the Christian community: 'Those who are in Judaea must take to the hills' (xiii, 14). Christians are involved in the apocalyptic catastrophe as individuals. The Jewish people are exposed to the *churban* as a people. Christians stand with one foot in the gentile camp. Jews are totally exposed.

The phrase 'when the Messiah comes' is not Biblical. Demythologised it means – with the breakdown of the old order the new one will arrive. 'The Day of the Lord' is a biblical phrase. The Apocalypse refers only to the hopeless catastrophe. The concept *churban* points also to the renewed and purified order, once again in God's Creation. 'When the Temple was destroyed, the Messiah was born', was the rabbinic consolation after the second *churban.*

In the rational age of Freud evil forces which are recognised by the religions as morally wicked, were only observed elements of the unconscious seeking blindly for outlets. Freud observed the hatred between the various nationalities of the decaying Austrian Empire. He observed 'fraternal hatreds'. But being a Jew, Freud was more occupied with the hatred of the son against the father. The Hungarians who hated the Slovaks, the German-speaking Austrians who hated the Czechs, were all involved in fratricidal strife. Patricide compared with fratricide lies even deeper in the subconscious layer of the mind. The antisemite in his hatred of the Jew hated not a living human being but a phantom, a figment of his imagination. The fantasy Jew of the antisemite is unconsciously seen as the 'bad' son, i.e. the rebellious son full of murderous wishes towards the father, and also as the 'bad' father, i.e. the potential torturer, castrator and killer of the son. In the midst of a rational age belief in evil spirits arose as it did in the age of which the above quoted words of the 'little Apocalypse' and of Rabbi Nehorai spoke. An exclusively rational age is not protected against insanity. Freud could heal individual patients. He could not heal his age, he was part of it.

The history of our age has led to an apocalyptic catastrophe. Is there meaning in the apocalyptic event? Guilt inherent in an age cries to heaven like the blood of Abel killed by Cain. There is a tradition within the Book of Genesis which makes Cain a city-builder; his descendants develop the various arts and crafts of a civilised community. Another tradition in the Book of Genesis describes Abel as the founder of a different kind of community, of one not burdened with guilt. An age need not end in apocalyptic disorder. If history remains connected with the world of the patriarchs, of fathers as they live in all ages, man can look forward with hope. Where on the other hand, history is reduced to a youth movement, men, young and old, are without any protection against dark powers, against the ruthless assault of irrational forces. Men who are creative in history need not be cut off from the world of the fathers as the Book of Genesis describes it. The goal of mankind's progress is not the horror of the apocalyptic end but the eternal return to the holy beginning. Father and son 'both walking together' (Genesis xxii, 6) are on the path which leads on to those chapters of history in which blessing is showered on mankind.

Where we search for God within history alone, we meet apocalyptic disorder. The young Buber called God 'the unity of the historic world'. Rosenzweig contradicted this view: such a god is the 'gigantic grave' of the men who believe in him and of the world which believers of this kind create. He is a dead god, a Moloch, a nothing. Rosenzweig sums up: 'We refuse to see "God in history"; we see God in every ethical enterprise within history but not in an imagined totality of history ... For Hegel history was god-like ... our opposition to the concept of history in the sense of the nineteenth century (Hegel and Hegel surviving in Marx) is our way of fighting for a religion fit for the twentieth century' (Letters, 55).

WERFEL'S CHRISTIAN
INTERPRETATION OF FREUD

I have written at length about Freud, yet I have not mentioned the myth of Oedipus. This story stands in the centre
of Freud's writing. I had no need to refer to this myth. I
have referred to Genesis ch. 22 and its Jewish, Christian
and Mohammedan exegesis. Father and son in unity, both
'walking together' – this is the Jewish reading. The father
allows the son to be sacrificed on the altar and yet remains
the loving father – this is the Christian reading. The father
sacrifices the son, the son has to obey – this is the Mohammedan reading. To the Muslim, God is a stern, tyrannical
father. Of the three possible father-son relationships Freud
knew only that of Islam. Islam itself he did not know. Unversed in the details of the three monotheistic religions, Freud
used the myth of Oedipus in order to say that a tyrannical
father brings misfortune to his family. Islam, as Semitic
Hellenism, sees God as the One who is nothing but ruler.
The Muslim is the slave of God. In the myth of Oedipus,
and equally in Islam, man does not have the freedom to
overcome fate.

Islam, the 'carrier' of Jewish and Christian piety, can
also be regarded as Jewish-Christian heresy, changing elements of Jewish and of Christian monotheism. A ruling
Church militant has features similar to Islam. A Constantinian Church, a Church with the aspiration of governing
secular affairs is near to Islam. The Church which Freud
saw in Vienna was a Church displaying that antisemitism
which Hitler later propagated in a similar, although more
radical, way. Freud always uses the word 'pious' and avoids
the word 'Christians'. From childhood on he had this ex-

perience: the Christians are the enemies of the Jews; his own enemies. Philosophically Freud was a child of the Enlightenment, which regarded any religion as an obstacle in the forward march of mankind. This obstacle will remain as long as the 'pious' stick to their illusions. In all this he repeated what the philosophy of enlightenment had taught before. It was impossible for Freud to realise his dependence on a past philosophy of rationalism which in its great representatives was more subtle and convincing than his shallow replica. He repeatedly said that philosophy was not for him. In fact, philosophy did not flourish in Freud's Vienna. Ilsa Barea in her remarkable book *Vienna* (Secker and Warburg, London, 1966) explained the absence of philosophy and the victory of positivism in Freud's Vienna. The reason was the lack of political freedom. It would have been impossible for Freud as member of Vienna University, to speak about Christianity in the radical way he did in his psycho-analytical essays, where he dealt generally with 'religion'. He seemed to be speaking about mental aberrations and about primitive pre-history, and what he said seemed to be in no way a direct attack on the dogma of the Church. The Austrian Church was satisfied with condemning psycho-analysis itself and Freud's 'theology' was not investigated. Freud himself would have denied the charge that he had attempted theology. But he had. The male leader of the horde being killed, patricide at the beginning of a new era, this concept was of immense theological importance. What the Christian theologian called deicide was described by Freud as patricide. The rise of Christianity begins as patricide. Sons leave their fathers and revolt against them.

Franz Werfel is the first of a large number of novelists who used Freud's writings as a kind of textbook. One of the examples from Freud's clinical material is exploited to provide a plot for the novelist. Freud himself went the other way: he read Goethe, Shakespeare, and Dostoevski, and used the material of these and other geniuses for general application. Werfel built a novel on Freud's understanding of the role of patricide, motivated by subconscious hatred, and eventually effecting a revolutionary change on the wider historical stage. The characteristic title of Werfel's novel is: *Nicht der Mörder, der Ermordete ist schuldig!* (Not the murderer, but the murdered victim is guilty.) It must be admitted that Werfel is different from those many writers whose dried-up imagination makes them turn to Freud to find there what they have not got in themselves. Werfel stands as an equal at the side of Freud, although the father-son conflict, described in his novel, is Freud's and not his copyright.

Werfel's novel displays a father-son conflict in two examples. The one example leads the reader into an upper middle class atmosphere. The father is a high army-officer who owes his successful career to nobody but himself, to his devotion to duty and self-denial. In his home he is the man in uniform, in the uniform of the superior who creates an unbearable tension in the family. Wife and son are overawed by the father. He is a father who intends to 'make' the son a success. He is more a master than a father.

The same situation is depicted in a lower class family. There the son really murders the father, whereas in the upper middle class family the hatred of the son does not lead to murder, but only to a scene in which the son threatens the old father with a pair of iron dumb-bells with which the father had in bygone years forced the son to do gymnastic exercises. The father had kept them in his wardrobe as a sentimental reminder of the time when his son had been a little boy and he a loving, though strict, father. The father sees in horror his own son turning against him as an attacker. Brandishing the dumb-bells as a weapon, the son chases the father, who runs away to save himself from his aggressor, his own flesh and blood. But no murder takes place. The son emigrates to America and by this action cuts himself off from his father. A father who never was a father and a son who was never given a chance to be a son depart from each other. In the parallel case where the murder did take place people try to solve the riddle why the father was murdered.

> *'The mother swears that there was*
> *never a quarrel between father and*
> *son. Anyway, the father always gave*
> *in, in a way the father had always*
> *a certain fear with regard to the son.*

> *"And the murderer himself? What*
> *does he say?" Nothing. He is silent.*
> *He shrugs his shoulders. We*
> *stand here before the sphinx of the*
> *human soul, before an insoluble mystery.'*

In this last sentence Werfel goes beyond Freud. For Freud there was no mystery, to him everything was clear.

Werfel tells the plot as a good novelist, who could be praised as a narrator. But the psychological insight is Freud's. He had discovered the possible existence of hatred where nothing else but love should be expected to prevail. To follow Freud into the psycho-analytical consequences of his discovery, is not our task. We are investigating the 'theologian' Freud, not the physician. Why should patricide have risen in Freud's eyes beyond the importance of a clinical case? Why should the story of the male leader of the horde have become so important to Freud in the face of the host of scholars who rejected this theory of the beginning of a new era? This question leads us to a psycho-analytical approach towards Freud himself. The biographical details of Freud's life are at our disposal. When he spoke about the 'pious', we said, he spoke about Christians. The Christians in Freud's Vienna were the enemies of the Jews. The Christian era is the 'new era', the new era begins with the murder – we have to quote again the story stubbornly defended by Freud – of the old male leader of the horde, killed by the sons. What the Christian Church calls deicide, appears to Freud as patricide. What happened at the moment of the rise of Christianity? Sons left their fathers, and more than that happened: patricide.

The Christian view of the patricidal separation of Christianity from Judaism is: 'Not the son, but the father is guilty.' The High Priest is guilty, the Sanhedrin is guilty, in fact the Jews are guilty. The bearded old Jews are guilty of the death of the son on the Cross. Werfel dramatises Freud's clinical discovery of patricide at the beginning of the new era and, changing Freud's facts, chooses as the title of his novel the words: 'Not the murderer, but the murdered victim is guilty.' Both Werfel and Freud speak of patricide. In patricide obviously the son is guilty. That is at least how Freud sees it, or – to be more correct – observes it. Werfel as a novelist is not an observer of facts but an interpreter. He interprets the patricide and changes Freud's fact into his: 'the son is not guilty, the murdered father himself is guilty'. Werfel has changed Freud's Jewish observation 'the father is the victim' into the Christian interpretation 'the son is the victim.'

Here lies the root of the difference between Judaism and Christianity which no dialogue can talk out of existence; it cannot be overcome through argument but only through kindness. Werfel takes side with the Christians and this is more important than whether he was baptised or – as is the case – never left the Jewish fold. Werfel accepts the Christian verdict that the Jews are responsible for the separation of the two monotheistic religions into the two hostile camps of Jews and Christians. Psychological analysis verifies that there are two hostile camps. What psychology observes, theology formulates, and does it in this way: The Jew will not surrender his conviction that truth is only one, and that it is the Jews who are shaped by the one truth into a nation. The Christian will not surrender his conviction that the separation from the Jews was necessary in the interest of the one truth which had to be brought to other nations who accepted the one truth, but remained nations. The rise of Christianity brought Judaism to the gentiles, and therefore the rise of Christianity was necessary.

Freud's observation of patricide is similar to Franz Rosenzweig's confrontation of Judaism with Christianity. Rosenzweig had never read a line of Freud when he wrote his main work *Der Stern der Erlösung,* and it is probable that Freud had never heard the name of Franz Rosenzweig. Yet there is an identity of views in these two great Jews. Rosenzweig speaks of the 'eternal youth' of the Christian, he sees Christianity as a kind of youth movement penetrating the old world of the gentiles. To them the Christians bring a new order. Sunday is the first day of the week on which the Christian gathers spiritual strength for his forward march into the world. The Sabbath is the seventh day of the week, when the Jew celebrates the perfect completeness of the Creation; it is the festival of Creation. Creation is the unchanging order. The fathers rule. History is the always new beginning, the sons go out and become creators themselves, building up – what? The tower of Babel, or Jerusalem? As Christians they hope to build Jerusalem, not the old Jerusalem of the fathers, but a new Jerusalem of the sons. There is only one God. But the one God worshipped by the fathers and the one God worshipped by the sons does not command the same commandments. 'Ye shall be holy' is not the commandment: Ye shall be spiritual. 'Love your neighbour' is a commandment differing from the commandment 'Love your enemies.' Jews and Christians are different. Creation on the one hand, and history with its Churches, cultures and civilisations on the other, are two different realms. But Jew and Christian, different as they are, are united in the hope that Creation can penetrate history and save history.

Freud looked into the depth of Creation, Rosenzweig into the depth of history. Both were Jews. At the side of these two Jews we see now a third speaker, this time a Christian: Bonhoeffer. From his Nazi prison he wrote letters to his fellow Christians and demanded a 'religionless Christianity'. With this Bonhoeffer is an equal of Rosenzweig and

Freud. Rosenzweig reminded his readers that the word 'religion' did not occur in the three volumes of *Der Stern der Erlösung*. Religion is organisation, is ritual; it can lead to God, but it can also distract from God. Rosenzweig became later a lover of Jewish rituals for reasons which make him today almost dated in this one respect and wrongly make him appear as a pietist ignoring prophetic Judaism. Rosenzweig whose thought will live on when the circumstances of German Jewry will only be understood by the specialist historian, was, as he himself said, not concerned with religion but with God, the Creator of heaven and earth. He was in this respect as Jew what Bonhoeffer was as a Christian.

At this point the question will be asked and asked with scepticism: How does Freud come in here at all? When we read his *Future of an Illusion* as the book of a writer talking the old language of the Enlightenment Movement, Freud is far removed from Rosenzweig and Bonhoeffer. But why identify Freud with what is only on the surface of what he wrote in this respect! Would not Rosenzweig and also Bonhoeffer have called the historical representations of all religions 'illusions'? What is of man-made fabric is not eternal. Anyone who believes that it is believes in an illusion. Only God is eternal. Did Freud say so? In so far as he was existentially a Jew, this was his belief. In so far as he expressed himself as a scientific writer, he was a child of his time, a son of Vienna, in which soon everything still valid, firm and even eternal in its appearance would prove to be an illusion. Vienna, the gay, golden Vienna of the old Emperor Franz Josef, would soon be the apparition of an illusion. In this respect Freud was right.

Freud was not merely a philosopher of bygone Enlightenment. He had deep religious insights. In the Austrian Roman Catholic Church which preached from its pulpits what Hitler later also preached, Freud discovered what he called the Oedipus Complex. He discovered the doings of the Constantinian Christian potentate who, as a father figure, was a father who would not love and could not be loved but could only be obeyed, as slave-drivers are obeyed by slaves. Freud also discovered what no German pupil of the Enlightenment or any follower of the French positivism of Comte would have been able to discover: the taboo ceremony. One must bear in mind all that the Christian theologian Rudolf Otto, author of the widely read and highly appreciated book *Das Heilige* (The Idea of the Holy) has to say about the experience in which what is holy is apprehended. Otto speaks of the *mysterium tremendum et fascinosum*. We feel ourselves attracted, mysteriously fascinated, and at the same time we feel we have to step back as if avoiding something dangerous. What is holy purifies man, and yet does it like the glowing coal which touches Isaiah's lips. The decisive point in all this is that man experiences a contact with a realm which transcends man. All that has been said by Otto about the category of the Holy, so different from the categories of the good and of the beautiful, is also said by Freud when he describes the taboo-meal. Both Rudolf Otto and Freud write as psychologists about man's experience of what he calls not 'good', 'true', or 'beautiful', but 'holy'. What Otto observes also on the higher civilised level, Freud observes first of all on the level of primitive, unrefined man. Both observe man's apprehension of what transcends man. For that neither Comte nor any German *Aufklärer* had an eye whereas Freud did.

He also knew that worship is sacrifice. He knew this because he observed man, the creature. What the creature 'knows' sometimes has stronger evidence than knowledge acquired through reason. Freud's observation of the taboo-character of the meal at which the communal sacrifice is eaten is – if we believe him as a scholar – derived from historians of primitive tribes and primitive ages. I do not doubt his sincerity as a scholar. But I doubt whether he is correct in regarding himself as a scholar in his observation of the taboo-meal. His observations are those of a Jew. Freud knew the Friday Evening and Eve-of-Festival-meal of the Jewish family. He reacted with the same disrespect as Anton Kuh, a man of Freud's Vienna who spoke of his fellow-Jews as his 'fellow-eaters and fellow-worshippers'. This judgment is a negative one. That does not diminish the importance of the observation. Before the animal sacrifice was supplanted by the spoken word, the prayer, mankind was able to make an even earlier progress. Sacrifice became a meal of the family, a meal eaten in the fellowship of man. What is primitive in this? It is a situation which is both human and holy. Instead of dragging the Jews down to a primitive status by ridiculing them as 'fellow-eaters and fellow-worshippers', we should rather see primitive man, as the Freudians call him, in an elevated status: he knows of worship and holiness, of fellowship; he knows, above all, that man is capable of communion with what transcends man. The situation is called 'primitive' because it is one which cannot be penetrated by the historian. Freud did not make his observations as a historian either. He made them in the subrational sphere. He only made the mistake of believing that in all this he was a scientist in the same way as one who works in the rational world of logic, mathematics and physics.

Freud has rightly been called the discoverer of a new continent; he discovered the sub-rational sphere of the human mind. But he is also an 'armchair anthropologist' who is a voracious reader of books about the primitive tribes. The facts on which he relied were in his time already out of date. The anthropologists who did field work in Freud's day are today proved to be erring pioneers. The 'primitives' whose taboo-meal Freud describes are in fact the Jews, as he sees them in his self-hatred, celebrating the Friday evening meal, and the 'pious' are the Christians celebrating holy communion. In the first case self-hatred, in the second his, the persecuted Jew's hatred of the Christians was the lamp which made visible what rested in the darkness of the unconscious: patricide and the category of taboo. Freud observed in the taboo situation what Otto called *mysterium tremendum et fascinosum*. The difference between holy and profane is not a product of civilised man, it is within man, the creature. Freud is an unwilling witness, but he is a convincing and important witness. Freud's depth-psychology describes man not as a product of culture and civilisation, but as he is after the 'neolithic evolution', when suddenly there is man distinguishing between holy and profane! The philosophy of positivism of the anthropologists speaks of neolithic evolution where the first stages of the Bible speak of the creation of man. For the anthropologist as for the Bible this is the beginning of man. What was before, the anthropologist cannot tell. For him too, the beginning is the miracle.

Freud's penetration of the sub-rational sphere of the mind sees the father-son conflict as a motive force in private life and in history. He discovers the murder of the father, patricide, 'the murder of the male leader of the horde' as the beginning of a new phase of history. To see patricide at the point in history which marks the beginning of Christianity may appear repulsive to a Christian. But this ugly picture has the virtue of endorsing the truth of Christianity. We do not possess historical facts about the first centuries of Christianity. The value of Freud's psycho-analytical approach to Christianity is therefore vitally important. It may appear repellent to a Christian to find the concept of deicide analysed and explained as patricide, just as it is repugnant to the Jew to have the patriarch identified with the 'old male leader of the horde'. A lake high in the Alps mirrors the surrounding trees and mountains. On a sunny day, especially at noon this lovely sight is spread out before us. But on a stormy day with a dark sky, the winds whipping up the mirror-like surface of the lake into choppy, darkish waves, how will the picture of the trees and mountains appear? Gone is the lovely image of the trees and mountains. But they will still be reflected there, and recognisable as what they are. In this way the rise of Christianity out of the Jewish people is recognisable as patricide. Freud's story of the patricide may appear ugly or rather terrifying, but in the same way as the gargoyles of a Gothic cathedral. Freud adds

132

the gargoyles to the Gothic cathedral of Christianity. This is not a distortion; the cathedrals, rising to spiritual heights, have their gargoyles. The medieval builders put them there, not as artists, but as Christians. Since not creative man, but man, the creature of God, contributed to the rise of Christianity, this rise was not an accident of history but a necessity. God, who chose the Jewish people to be His messenger, has also chosen the Christians. There are two elections, both different from each other, but both valid elections.

Freud wrote as a Jew. That does not mean that he wrote consciously about Judaism or Christianity. The very difference between Judaism and Christianity did not concern him much. To him both were only 'religions', but there was an important difference between them. Christianity was the religion of the enemy. It is advisable to know your enemy, to observe everything about him. It is important for your safety and protection. This is the reason why Freud could make important statements of a theological nature. The object of observation is outside. Christianity was outside, and Freud was a good observer. The persecuted needs must be a careful observer of the persecutor.

I have so far not mentioned what Freud calls 'the death-wish'. Some readers of Freud will think that his view about man's death-wish is derived from observation of pathological facts. There is the host of Freudians who have not yet discovered the whole Freud. Writing about the death-wish Freud discovers the heart of the Christian who longs for redemption. (see pp. 87–88) We have spoken of the authentic sin which is the sin of any moral transgression, of the imaginary sin which is a symptom of the sickness of mind, and the sin which the Christian calls original sin. Man aspiring to rise to spiritual heights remains rooted in the secular sphere. Even somebody who is a saint in the Christian view is chained to the secular world. Of his chains only death can finally redeem him. The doctrine of original sin makes Christianity a religion in which redemption is the central aim. Freud, facing the doctrine of original sin and of redemption, speaks with the objection of the Jew. He speaks of the death-wish. As a Jew, Freud 'knew' what holy means, although he called it taboo. But he did not know what 'spiritual' meant.

In Hebrew there is only one word for both 'know' and 'love'. One only knows what one observes with love. Freud lacked the love which would have explained to him what the Christian doctrine of original sin and redemption meant. He used the word 'death-wish'. Although it is a word from the world of an atheist, it should not be regarded as useless for two reasons. First, the 'atheist' Freud was still the Jew shaped by the prayer: 'The soul which Thou hast given me is pure.' Secondly, Christianity as the religion of the sons rises into the spiritual sphere. In the noble torment of the awakening youth spiritual forces struggle and try to shape the character of the future adult. The psychological situation of any adolescent is beset with problems. In this age group flourishes idealism, readiness for sacrifice, in short, the readiness for spiritual existence. If this age group marches forward under wrong guidance, they may even be guided by a death-wish and refuse to grow up. The suicide rate of the young and mentally diseased is the sign of our uprooted civilisation. Spiritual man is, must be, uprooted. This is his vocation and his danger. The Christian is uprooted from the secular sphere. Christianity is healthy when it is rooted in the Jewish faith in which the distinction between holy and profane does not devalue the profane and so allows spiritual works and spiritual life to grow from the blessed soil of the perfect Creation.

As Jews, Schnitzler, Werfel, Kraus and the numerous Jewish intellectuals and artists of Vienna were not different from Freud. Where was their Judaism that held them back from baptism? It is an unfair answer to say they were neither Jews nor Christians but liberals, believing in the progress which would one day bring freedom, bring the *Weg ins Freie* (Exodus into Freedom), as Schnitzler called one of his novels. Judaism in the profoundest sense can in the last resort never be reduced to a creed. Judaism is a form of human existence.

We can best explain what the Jew is through the type of the father. The family, the father with his wife and children, represents the life of man created by God. The family is a holy order. The existence of a Jew is holy and human. This holy humanity was the contribution made by Freud and his fellow-Jews in Austria. Freud was surrounded in Vienna by hatred. Germans, Czechs, Magyars, Slovaks, Poles, Italians all hated each other, and were all antisemites. As Roman Catholics they were Christians of the medieval pattern. Leadership was in the hands of a decadent aristocracy and of an equally decadent Church. The Church taught the doctrine of infallible leadership. This became a secularised dogma serving Hitler well. It has been said that the Jews were the only people who were loyal to the Hapsburg Empire, in fact, it can be said that they were the only people who remained human in a world of hatred, decadence and orgiastic gaiety. In this Roman Catholic carnival Austria waltzed with a murderer. Austria gave birth to Hitler and brought him up.

The humanity, characteristic of Jewish existence enabled Freud to discover the innocence of the whole created world, which includes the great world of the unconscious. Freud's psycho-analysis was Jewish. Sin is mistake, even pathological aberration, but never a 'must-sin' (Buber). The dogma of original sin did not frighten Freud. God, according to a phrase in the Jewish prayer book, is a 'faithful physician'. Freud, the discoverer of patricide, knew what the true function of a father is: to bring peace. The Hebrew word for peace, *shalom* has the same root as the word *shalem* which means 'whole'. To be whole is to enjoy health. As the bringer of peace the father is a healer.

Only two examples of the humanity of the Jews in Freud's Vienna will be mentioned: Schnitzler's play *Professor Bernhardi* and Karl Kraus' poem *The Dying Soldier*. Professor Bernhardi refuses a Roman Catholic priest permission to perform the last rites for a girl who is experiencing euphory in the last hour of her life. She is convinced she is now cured of her tuberculosis and will soon leave

135

hospital in perfect health. The Jewish physician protects the happiness of his patient. The Roman Catholic priest has only his duty as the son of his Church in mind. He would like to perform the last rites and so rob the girl of her last happy hours in life. The clash between the Jewish physician and the Roman Catholic priest becomes a conflict mirroring two different worlds. Which is right, the humanity of the Jew, or the spirituality of the priest?

Karl Kraus' poem has so far proved to be untranslatable into English. The following transposition into prose must serve instead of a translation, of which only a poet of the greatest stature would be capable:

> *Captain, order a court martial!*
> *I am not prepared to die for a Kaiser!*
> *Captain, you are the Kaiser's hireling!*
> *When I am dead, I shall salute no more!*
>
> *When my place is at the side of my Lord*
> *The Kaiser's throne will be beneath me,*
> *And I shall scorn all his commands.*
> *Where is my village? My son plays there.*
>
> *When I am asleep in the bosom of my Lord,*
> *My last letter from the front will arrive.*
> *The call of love, profound and strong*
> *Goes out from my heart and will be heard.*
>
> *Captain, you are out of your mind*
> *To have sent me hither.*
> *My heart is consumed by fire.*
> *I die, but not for a fatherland.*
>
> *You cannot force me, you cannot force me!*
> *See, how death breaks the chains.*
> *You can do nothing but court martial death.*
> *I die, but not for a Kaiser!*

This is a Jewish poem, full of feeling for the suffering soldiers. Kraus sees the martyr in the hero. Kraus' *The Last*

Days of Mankind about the ordeals of the years 1914–1918 does not deal with strategy and politics, but with the men in the trenches who were driven to death. Kraus refuses to be silent about the tragedy. He cries out that there is no way out: 'Before us the enemy, behind us the fatherland.' Kraus describes as chronicler of the First World War the misery of the suffering creature of God. The blood spilt by Cain cries to heaven. Above all his poem *The Dying Soldier* with the line 'I shall die, but not for a Kaiser', is the challenge to a Constantinian Christianity still alive in the covenant between 'Throne and Altar'. This poem has nothing to do with pacifism. The Austrian Jews, like the German Jews, were patriots and full of that enthusiasm with which the youth of Europe marched off in August 1914 to its Golgotha. The most beautiful war-poem written in German *The Soldier's Grave* was written by a Jew, Hugo Zuckermann, like Karl Kraus an Austrian. Pacifism is a political device. Those who preach peace are something else and more than pacifists.

Freud and all these gifted and less gifted Jewish writers and artists, journalists, physicians and lawyers in Austria and Germany are not with their humane contribution to their gentile surroundings, to be understood as humanists. They were Jews. The gentiles rush towards the stage of history, keen to create. The Jew happily joins them, but as a Jew he is a man created by a history which God had created. The humanist is the noble gentile. But Christian and humanist are rooted in and guided by their gentile history. The Jew has a history in which God created him to be a Jew. Freud and those like him were Jews without Torah, which means without the knowledge of their own history as created by God the Creator of the world. Of this Creation-within-history, to which words like Sinai, Exodus, Covenant, *Torah* point, the Jew is an offspring. He is what the rabbinic term 'son of man' expresses, a man who, whether learned or simple, brings the gifts of God to man. Freud, the healer, Karl Kraus, the mouthpiece of the soldier sent to his death, Schnitzler providing a few happy hours for the sick girl – each of these

137

Jews, cut off from the knowledge of the *Torah,* from the knowledge of their holy history which made each of them – is still a Jew. Jewish humanity may, but need not exist without the refinement of the humanist. But Jewish humanity has power and warmth. The gentile humanist can fall back into gentile coldness, even into the gentile lack of mercy and love. This cannot happen to the Jew, who is never given a chance by God to withdraw into a gentile status.

The humanist is a creator: He creates. In activity and in contemplation he remains a creator. His noble achievements and his limitations are thus explained. We may praise his achievements and point to his limitations. Both are possible. With the humanity of the Jew it is different. In him we must praise the Creator who performs a second act of creation within history. The Jew is God's creation. As God's creation within history the Jew is second creation – 'son of man' who is the child of God. As son of man, with all the marks of the creature on him, the Jew in the midst of history is like the world itself created by God.

The historian who praises the circle around Freud for making Vienna the Athens on the Danube must not forget the Jews in the poorer quarters of Vienna, the *Leopoldstadt,* who displayed the same humanity in their misery and shabbiness as did the Jewish writers and artists who contributed to the fame of imperial Vienna. Whether well-placed in refined and civilised surroundings or suffering in a barbaric environment, the Jew with his fate makes the gentiles face God. The gentiles meet in the Jew – to use again the Biblical and rabbinic expression – 'the son of man', the God-made creature within history. In this sense we can say: The Jew-baiters, the Jew-killers are guilty of deicide. We can demythologise the word 'son of god.' With the phrase 'son of man' who is 'son of God' we express the faith in God-in-man. 'The word is very nigh unto thee, in thy mouth and in thy heart' (Deuteronomy xxx, 14). But as the word of God has authority and equally transcends the human subject of faith, the phrase 'out there' should not be dismissed as quaint and old-fashioned, as is done by the Bishop of Woolwich. God who resides 'very nigh' is beyond man and beyond everything of which man knows. He is, indeed, 'out there'.

For decades the plan for the killing of the Jews had been prepared in Austria. Before the 'male leader of the horde' was brought to his doom in the Berlin bunker, he did the killing himself. The allegation that 'Austria was overrun by Germany' is a historical lie comparable to the other historical lie of the 'stab in the back' of a victorious Germany in World War I. From Austria, from this antisemitic Vienna which made Hitler, came the poison which transformed Germany into Nazi Germany. Only the Bavarians were right from the beginning the equals of the Austrians in Germany. The Austrian Roman Catholic Church was the most decadent, the most reactionary of the Christian Churches: after 1918 a Roman Catholic priest was reprimanded because he had criticised the injustice of *ius primae noctis*. The Austrian Roman Catholic Church was still the Constantinian Church in the twentieth century. She preserved in the alliance of Throne and Altar the Constantinian potentate who either as pope or as Kaiser was the 'male leader of the horde'. Grown old, weak, but all the more cruel he retained in his hands the power which guided towards no mission. 'The kings of the world are old and will have no heirs,' diagnosed Rilke. But Freud saw everywhere, albeit with the help of abstruse anthropological theories, the ugly face of the 'male leader of the horde'. He tramped through the streets of Vienna, and his name was Hitler. The antisemitic sermons of the Austrian Roman Catholic clergy who spread the belief in Jewish ritual murder and incensed in this and other ways Jew-hatred among the mob, prepared the way for Hitler. The cry *'Heil Hitler'* and the curse 'Perish Judah' were not different from the antisemitic sermons preached in Austrian Roman Catholic Churches. Vienna was once a Protestant city, but all vestiges of the Reformation were destroyed in fire and blood. Old people in Vienna still use the phrase, no longer understood by many: 'I shall make you a Catholic'

139

(*Ich werde dich katholisch machen*). Small children who hear it spoken by an old nanny or a rough schoolmaster are frightened. They know the phrase means they are in for merciless treatment; they will be beaten into the change which *Herr Stock* (master stick) demands. Austria is the country in which Nazism was born. The Prussian obedience of anyone who commands as master, militarism as the essence of German philosophical idealism, made Hitlerism fatally successful. But Germany made amends after the war, convicted murderers, paid restitution. Austria does not do much of this kind. They invented the historical lie 'we were overrun by Germany'! The Austrians have not changed. In 1966, twenty-one years after the world heard about Auschwitz and the other concentration camps, in an Austrian monastery nuns still display relics which they tell the visitors are those of a child murdered by Jews, who need Christian blood for their Passover Festival.

Part Four:

THE MONOTHEISTIC OECUMENE

JEWISH FELLOWSHIP

'Until August 1914 a sensible, law-abiding Englishman could pass through life and hardly notice the existence of the state, beyond the post office and the policeman ... Unlike the countries of the European continent, the state did not require its citizens to perform military service' (A. J. P. Taylor, *English History 1914–1945*). In Germany the state pervaded private life. Hegel's deification of the state was the philosophical justification of this situation. Yet it was Hegel himself who distinguished between state and *Gesellschaft* (society). Hegel created the terminology in which state and society differ from each other. The thinkers who succeeded Hegel carved up his philosophical system according to their choice between an affirmation of the state or of society. The Hegelian Left', led by Karl Marx, ignored the state, the 'Hegelian Right' ignored society. In Germany shaped by Prussia and in Metternich's Austria the Hegelian Right won the day. Marx's hope that the state would 'wither away' was Jewish messianism and English pragmatism which were both quickly brushed aside by the Russian marxists. A totalitarian state suppresses the *Gesellschaft,* society.

About the same time as the German Jew Hugo Preuss wrote the constitution of what was later to be called the Weimar Republic and which lasted up to 1933, Franz Rosenzweig wrote his *Stern der Erlösung*. Hugo Preuss's desire was to establish the *Rechtsstaat,* a state entirely based on justice. In his *Stern,* Rosenzweig recognised this desire as Jewish messianism and stressed that a state is a state only when it wields power. The state has to dispense justice but its first step is to reach for power. With this double function of administering social justice and political power, the state is preserved from totalitarianism but remains a state. Hugo Preuss, the Jew, ignored the element of power and left the state defenceless in the hour of crisis. Communists and fascists and, above all, the Nazis ignored justice and robbed man of his humanity. As long as the Messiah is still to come society needs the armour of the state to survive. The state, on the other hand, interfering in all the private aspects of social life is – Leviathan, a monster breeding monsters.

The difference between society and state, between social and political life, can be seen in human affairs. In peacetime society flourishes; during wars civil life is restricted and curtailed, and the state dictates. The life which is described in the patriarchal stories of the Book of Genesis is social life. Birth and death, wooing and marrying, working in order to have bread, craving for the blessing of the good life – that is the content of patriarchal life. We should speak of the life of the 'fathers' rather than of the 'patriarchs', 'fathers' is the correct translation of the Hebrew word *abot*. The Greek word 'patriarch' no longer makes it clear that each living generation hails from the 'fathers'. Patriarchs can and do live at any time. The life of the fathers is the life of man as the creature of God. It is not life on the level of creative man, nor is it life reduced to the mere satisfaction of hunger. It is not the life of man who is now called 'economic man'. It is the life of man who, as we see in the Old Testament, speaks with God 'mouth to mouth' (Numbers xii, 8). Abraham, Isaac and Jacob, who meet God, live outside the state. The Pharaoh of the Book of Exodus is still far off. In whichever way the meeting with God can be described in the lives of Abraham, Isaac and Jacob, it takes place in a privacy not interfered with by political influence. There is nothing of the state in the life of the fathers. Read the Book of Genesis, and see the holiness of life outside the state!

To see the grandeur of creative man, we look to Athens and its free democracy. There we admire the orator, the philosopher and the soldier, the men who are the guardians

144

of the city (*polis*). We do not see any women. They are in the background. They, like the slaves, have no standing in the political gatherings of the men. These men always move in public life. Their life in the family appears to be without interest for the Greek writers who concentrate their observations on public life alone. Families are noble or belong to the lower class. Family life as such is not experienced in the way of the Book of Genesis. The ladies of Periclean Athens were dignified matrons, philosophising mistresses of famous men, pretty girls. They were in no way similar to Sarah, Rebeccah, Leah and Rachel. Eros was praised by the poets also in homosexual relationships. Love which is 'strong as death' was not discovered, nor was the holiness which mother-hood bestows on the simplest of women. The men retained a boyishness in their adult lives. Games had the character of worship, freedom was the property of a ruling class. Art was honoured, so was the soldier's role, manual labour was the lot of slaves. Athens meant imperialism, but – it must not be forgotten – also moderation. Of course, slavery remains slavery and is not affected by one or even by a thousand men being kind to their slaves. Athens as a democracy was not identical with the totalitarian state, as Plato visualises it in his *Politeia*. The *tyrannis,* the no longer typically Greek but more oriental state with its despotism brought an end to Greek glory.

The geography of Palestine is adverse to the establishment of an enduring state. The geographical situation made allowance only for a buffer state, and this only in interim periods. The Davidi and Maccabean states were comparatively short intervals in the four millennia of Biblical and post-Biblical Jewish history. The Jewish people preserved itself more as a social than as a political entity. Eventually Jewish law faced as a social law the political law of the Roman state. The ideals of a society are those of private life: justice, litigation by negotiation, the settlement of differences by persuasion; to sum it all up in the words of the prophet: 'Not by might, nor by military power, but by

My spirit, saith the Lord of hosts' (Zechariah iv, 6). The ideals of the state are the very things which the prophet rejects: military power bringing victory, and no falling back exclusively on persuasion and bargaining.

The reality of life does not clearly distinguish state from society. In normal times only philosophers and sociologists work out a typology with state and society as unmixed and absolutely different opposites. But the times through which we have gone in the two world wars were not normal times. What we have experienced is the rise of the naked state and the catastrophe of that society which in its entirely unarmed existence is most characteristic of non-political social life: the catastrophe of the Jewish people on the European continent. This happened at a time when Jews had become westernised and had as soldiers served the state with the distinction of the heroes of Thermopylae. But to the totalitarianism of the Nazis the Jews remained suspect. As a people living the non-political life of a society shaped by prophets and rabbis the Jews were regarded as enemies of the state. This they were not.

Christians, not Jews, are chosen to fight the state. The State-Church controversy is the glory of medieval Christendom and made the western world a community of free men. Jews are differently chosen: they have to sanctify society. The Church transforms political values into spiritual values. The Jews transform profane life into holy life. Spiritualisation is aggressive. It suppresses a part of life. What is secular is not only not Christian, it is a contradiction of Christianity. Sanctification, on the other hand, does not devalue profane life. Out of the profane is cut out what is holy. The word 'temple' is derived from the Greek word *temnein* which means 'to cut out'. A special place is cut out of life and destined for sanctification. The Jewish people, chosen to be a 'holy people', is cut out from the midst of the people of the state, from the midst of the gentiles. What is holy must not be used for the purposes of ordinary life. An animal, once dedicated for future sacrifice in the Temple, must no longer be used by the farmer for work in the field. As a 'holy people' we serve in history, but we do not serve in history alone. The Nazis who wanted to make history without God, could not but see the Jews as their enemies representing society, holy and profane. Of course, Christians, too, were enemies of the Nazi state. Hitler knew it from the beginning. Christians did not realise their proper role towards Nazism sufficiently or realised it only late. The Nazi state contradicted both what is holy and what is spiritual, opposed society and Church, Jew and Christian.

It is the outcome of a muddled theology, in fact the outcome of a lack of theological clear thinking, to speak of 'secular Judaism' in the same way in which we are entitled to speak of secularised Christianity. A Church on becoming secularised falls back into its pre-Christian origin: it becomes a state. The evidence of history supports this fact. Rome, once the name heralding the imperial power of the Caesars, became the Rome of the Popes. This historical change from one Rome to another Rome is the change from a political into a spiritual institution. As the state can become a Church, can become spiritualised, so too a Church can become secularised. Only to a Church can this change from a spiritual status into a secularised one apply. It cannot apply to society. It cannot apply to Jewish life either. One cannot speak of a secularised Judaism.

As the Church has a close affinity to the state, so has Jewish life an affinity to a society, which can have sanctification and can lose it. The loss of sanctification is not a secularisation but is a falling back into profanity. But profane life is still the life of the creatures of God. It is still in the midst of the God-created world. 'Profane' does not mean bad or wicked, it means what the word says, *profanum,* 'outside the temple', outside sanctified life. Profane life can be shallow, even vulgar, but it is without the stigma of the depravity of the secularised Christian who is a demoniac type. He once had the ambition of conquering heaven, and retaining this ambition turns now to another conquest. What conquest can this be? A man who has once seen the light of heaven, sees nothing outside heaven. Secularised spiritual man can become a demoniac nihilist. Nietzsche knew this. 'Who once has lost what thou hast lost cannot stand still', he said of European man, who, as secularised Christian, moved towards nihilism.

Amid the sickness of Europe on the precipice of nihilism, the Jew remained healthy and spread health. As a Jew he was impervious to nihilism. It is often a Christian mistake to regard the Jew burning with prophetic criticism as a nihilist. But Jewish criticism is positive, conservative in the strictest sense; it has the aim of bringing back to a solid start from God's good Creation creative man who has gone astray. Modern Jewry may have lost to some degree, even to a high degree, its rituals, its separateness from the gentiles, its pietistic culture, but this is not secularisation. In sanctification profane life is acknowledged and praised as the gift of God, as the Creation of God. When we say the Jewish benediction, the bread remains bread and the wine remains wine. When a modern Jew stops saying these blessings, he is still a Jew, the human product of sanctified life, even if he has lost the knowledge of what made him a Jew before he was born. Becoming involved in the profane life, he does not become demoniac.

Simone Weil found it impossible to enter the Church; she remained, with her praise of 'all secular life' a true Jewess: 'There are so many things outside it (the Church); so many things that I love and do not want to relinquish; so many things that God loves, or else they would not exist. The whole immense vista of past centuries ... all the countries inhabited by the coloured races; *all secular life in the white people's countries;* and in the history of those countries all the traditions banned as heretical – the Manichaean and Albigensian, for example; and all the things that came out of the Renaissance, too often degraded, but not altogether without value.' (*Waiting on God*, pp. 26–27, my italics.) She could not see her true fatherland either in the state or in the Church, and writes: 'The children of God ought not to have any other fatherland below except the universe itself, with the totality of all the reasoning creatures it ever has contained, contains, or ever will contain. That is the native city to which we owe our love' (ibid., pp. 43–44).

The loss of the medieval ritualism has in fact not changed the Jew. Situated less in the political and more in the social sector of gentile life the modern Jew, the western Jew could preserve his Jewish existence. His change from his medieval habitat to his modern situation meant no secularisation. It meant no existential change at all. Again the Hegelian distinction between state and society has to be remembered. It is valid even when so much of Hegel's philosophy has become out of date. To be ready for the requirements of the state, a change was necessary in Jewish life. The Jew had to become a soldier. That had not been required of him since the end of the Maccabean State. The people of the Diaspora has been for two millennia, from Massada to Ben Gurion, a people without an army. This will not change as far as the majority of the Jewish people, living outside Israel, is concerned. That the Jew could become a soldier at all, was possible because in the West the soldier is a citizen-soldier. The citizen-soldier is a citizen armed for the duration of the war. Duty, this social virtue, and not the political ideal of heroism makes him a good soldier. The verse which schoolboys have been taught for so long, 'It is sweet to die for the fatherland', is not for him. Loss of freedom and denial of justice are worse than death. Thus the citizen becomes a warrior. From the post-medieval working population rise the types of bourgeois, intellectual and citizen-soldier, and the Jew joins these non-political figures. He has a place in the community which economic necessities have brought together. They are not of a spiritual nature, but are the necessities of man as the creature of God. The Jew sees the non-Jew as a creature of God and joins him in fellowship. The Jew is different from men shaped by political and spiritual aims. Yet he is not antagonistic towards them.

149

It is only the Promethean urge in the gentiles which creates the difference between gentile and Jew.

The modern Jew finds his place in the social sector of life where he can be a Jew. The talmudist who becomes a modern lawyer is not a secularised Jew. He has not even entered a profane life. Law in any form as law of justice is the law of God. The profession of the lawyer, of the physician, of the teacher, are priestly professions. By flocking into these professions Jews do not become secularised, have not entered profane life. They were able to preserve a priestly existence in the midst of modern society. Where the state leaves room for non-political society, Jews have a place and a function and can uphold their mission.

It is today more necessary than ever to know what it really means when a whole class is called 'bourgeois'. The working class of the West has economically moved up into the bourgeois sphere. With the achievement of social security, the working class received its admission-ticket to the bourgeois class. But the word bourgeois has retained its derogatory meaning. The bourgeois is not a soldierly type, nor is he an artist. Artists, especially when not successful, give their public the bad name of bourgeois. A defence of the bourgeois from the Christian camp is never to be expected. The bourgeois, with his feet on the ground, does not have the spiritual features of ascetic spirituality.

Were the Nazis right, when they identified bourgeois and Jew? This question can be answered by another question: is the bourgeois a God-believing man? Sometimes he is, sometimes he is not. If he is not, he is according to Tillich 'finiteness resting in itself'. The same low opinion about the bourgeois is held by Mlle. Daumard who writes about the French bourgeoisie (Adeline Daumard: *La bourgeoisie parisienne de 1815–1848,* Paris; Oxford, Parker) 'They were rationalists, though not disinclined to cherish religion for its social benefits, yet "God was not dead"; he had merely removed himself from the thoughts and the habitual behaviour of the bourgeois.' What Tillich and Mlle. Daumard say about the bourgeois has in exactly the same way been said about Islam which was regarded as being not a monotheistic religion but merely a 'Semitic Hellenism'. Tillich and Mlle. Daumard could be right, if the bourgeois were only a bourgeois and entirely without his former Jewish or Christian heritage. The Jewish bourgeois was a Jew, and could more easily remain a Jew than the Christian bourgeois could remain a Christian. The bourgeois is as different from Jew and Christian as the pious Mohammedan obeying the Law of the Koran is. It must not be forgotten that the law-abiding Mohammedan belongs to the monotheistic family. Islam can, as a monotheistic religion, be called a religion of reason and duty. Accordingly, the bourgeois, nominally a Christian, can often be viewed as a Mohammedan outside historical Islam. Such a view is without any derogatory meaning. Islam is a great and powerful form of monotheism.

If the bourgeois is a God-believing man, he is nearer to the Jew than to the Christian. Kierkegaard called the patriarchal stories a 'bourgeois idyll'. A bourgeois is a Jew without the Jewish election. The German bourgeoisie was in the Nazi years not persecuted like the Jews. They could – and did – wear the swastika. The Jewish bourgeois can remain a true Jew by upholding the role of the father in the family. This role is denied to man by the totalitarian state which establishes in the *Führer* a father-image in place of the real father. The real, loving father who honours in woman the child of God and leads his children towards the good life has no longer any say when the political father-figure is in command. The Jew is bidden to be a *baal-habayit*, the priestly father of his family. The anti-bourgeois animosity directed against the gentile bourgeois is in a way an antisemitism directed against gentiles. It is hostility against those who have been bred by peace and live in peace. It is the hostility of those who have chosen a life without peace, the hostility of spiritualists, artists and soldiers who are not citizen-soldiers but praise war unconditionally as a heroic enterprise.

A German islamist has coined the term 'carrier of religion'.

Islam is not Judaism or Christianity, but as a 'carrier of religion' it can be a carrier of Jewish or Christian values. We can turn with the term 'carrier of religion' to the bourgeois who can be a carrier of Judaism or Christianity. But, being based on reason and morality and not transcending them, bourgeois life, though never identical with Jewish life has a greater affinity to Judaism than to Christianity. There is no spirituality in bourgeois life. But it has access in the non-political life of the family to that sanctification without which Jewish life is not Jewish.

The age following the French Revolution was a bourgois age in which the Jews experienced a renaissance similar to the one at the time of the flourishing of Islam. Marx, Freud, Franz Rosenzweig – to name only these three among the hundreds who could be named – came from bourgeois families. Has the bourgeois age now reached its end? The end of bourgeois life and the end of intellectual existence would mean the proletarianisation of tycoon and wage-earner alike, so that all would fall victim to the mass-age. Who are the first to be eliminated by the totalitarian state? It is the bourgeois and the intellectual! Not every bourgeois is a father who makes the family a holy unity; not every intellectual is a prophet. But to the bourgeois and the intellectual the term 'carrier' of Jewish or Christian values is applicable. However different the bourgeois as a suburban type and as a well-paid worker from the bourgeois of early capitalism, he can still create a home for his wife and his children. The intellectual as a modern writer, speaking as an official ombudsman, is different from the intellectuals of Voltaire's age who were aristocrats, but he can still act like an Old Testament prophet, rejecting the superiority of state and Church. Of course the bourgeois appears to be defeated by the Russian Commissar and the Western organisation man. But what once flourished in our Judaeo-Christian civilisation can never perish. The feudal age, for instance, is dead, but the knight (gentleman) and the priest remain irreplaceable figures of Western society. A similar rehabilitation is due to the bourgeois. The West is the bourgeois West.

The Jew as bourgeois and as intellectual can be the 'carrier' of true Jewish forms of life. The Jew always has a mission in the Christian world. In a world of secularised Christianity – which some misleadingly call a post-Christian world – this Jewish mission is beneficial to mankind. It does not rob Christianity of its mission to convert the gentiles. The Jewish mission is a mission to bring blessing. The Jew himself, being what he is, does not undergo the change which is the consequence of secularisation, although his lot is seriously affected by the secularisation of the Christian world around him. In this secularised civilisation of ours, in this so-called 'post-Christian' world, the great hour of Judaism strikes. At this time of the greatest persecution of the Jewish people begins the hour of the Jew, the hour of the Jewish faith. For the sake of a re-Christianisation of the secularised world, Christians will do well to look to their origin in Judaism.

Not only the state, culture too emancipates itself from the Church in the process of secularisation. This process led to the autonomous state and to an autonomous culture, in fact to autonomous man, who was rightly hailed as the modern, i.e. post-medieval, man representing our Western world. But autonomy as independence from the Church is one thing; the autonomy which rejects the law of God, rejects God, is another matter. The struggle for an autonomous civilisation has been fought out. This struggle is the past of Western man, as far back as the French Revolution. The way to a new theonomy is before us. This is our future, if we are to survive. We have to get away from the nihilism to which totalitarianism, the still-prevailing exclusive affirmation of political values, leads. The humanist belief in cultural values alone also ends in nihilism. The Renaissance dream of replacing holiness by beauty is over. We have the evidence of German history before us: 'From humanism to nationalism, from nationalism to bestiality.' This is the warning of the Austrian poet Grillparzer (1791–1872), who alludes to the *Beast* of the Apocalypse.

The exclusive affirmation of political values is no temptation for the Jew, certainly not for the Jew outside Israel, but nor is it so for the Israeli. His is the humanist temptation, the exclusive affirmation of cultural values. It is to be hoped that Bonhoeffer's saying the 'world has come of age' refers also to us Jews and that we shall free ourselves from the fascination which swayed German Jews and made them see Goethe's writings as their Bible. But German Jews themselves returned with Franz Rosenzweig to their origin in the Hebrew Bible. Professor Erich Heller is mistaken when he believes that '. . . whether . . . in London or in . . . San Francisco, the Modern Mind speaks German, not always good German but fluent German nonetheless!' If he had written 'the nineteenth-century mind' instead of 'the Modern Mind' he would be half way to the truth. But the nineteenth century is over and done with. As Professor Heller still clings to the German nineteenth century about which as a German-teacher at English and American universities he publishes many essays, no wonder that he clamours about the 'Disinherited Mind', and chooses this pronouncement of despair as the title of one of his books. Heller writes exactly in the old way of a *Kultur-Jude*. He reports, for instance, Goethe's idea for a reformed education and his suggestion to have the Cross veiled in order not to inflict psychological harm on young children. At this point Heller expresses his civilised protest about such an affront against the dominating faith. He has nothing to say either from a Jewish or from a Christian point of view. He remains faithful to his exclusively aesthetic valuation.

The Biblical philosophy of Franz Rosenzweig views the whole secularised age and reminds us that not only the state, but culture too, offers no absolute. Where culture is expected to render revelation, the German *Kultur* leads to that nihilism which the prophets saw as the danger when they castigated the idols, the *ellilim,* the nothings. Jeremiah x, 14

154

identifies the 'nothing' with deceit of the heart, with illusion. Beauty, which the European Renaissance substituted for holiness, is no longer attractive, since Hollywood has manufactured it on a conveyor belt. *Kultur,* after emigrating from bourgeois Germany to America, has found a place in magazines and in the colour supplements of Sunday papers. Mass-produced beauty, used as a dope for man who lives the ant-life of the crowd, has become boring. But even at the height of German culture the philosophers who, as romantics, enhanced beauty as the highest value, did not influence Jewish thinking. Heine, as a poet, not as a thinker, had his spell of romanticism. He soon turned with dismay against political romanticism. From Moses Mendelssohn to Franz Rosenzweig everyone who spoke as thinker, as intellectual or as preacher for German Jewry saw justice, not beauty, as the springboard to the transcendental world. Beauty which does not radiate goodness cannot speak to the human heart.

'Samaria and her idols' (Isaiah x, 11), the 'goldsmith and his molten image' (Jeremiah, x, 14), art, *Kultur* are rejected as media of revelation, just as the state is rejected by Zechariah's 'not by military power' (iv, 6) as the place of God's glory. A 'Jewish' culture as a substitute for Judaism is rejected by the Biblical prophet, and a Jewish state is not Jewish. Martin Buber is a believer in Jewish culture, Franz Rosenzweig is not. The latter warned the connoisseurs of art, 'When art alone builds culture, it does not create a home for man'. The stage is not the world. In German *Kultur* the world was made a stage. The last act was the *Götterdämmerung*. Rosenzweig does not allow the difference between prophet and creative genius to become blurred. Judaism has made a great contribution to civilisation. This proves that the Islamic rejection of art was not the way of Jewish monotheism. Jew, Christian and Mohammedan, however different they may be in the principles of their theism, agree that art, just like the state, when raised to the status of the Absolute, leads to nihilism.

155

What Franz Rosenzweig says about the 'nothing' is in harmony with the medieval philosophy of Maimonides concerning the negative attributes of God. Of God, Maimonides teaches, we can only say what He is not. He is not man. He is not any form. Maimonides, it seems at first, comes very near to the nihilistic doctrine: God is nothing. That was the case with the anti-mythology of Aristotle which led to the fall of the Greek gods. Maimonides was saved from an Aristotelian denial of the positive attributes of God by his adherence to prophetic teaching.

The prophets avail themselves of certain positive attributes of God. God is King. God is father. These images are permissible. Permissible in their application to God are the images of the love of the child towards the father, of the love of the father towards his child, of the love between bridegroom and bride, of the love between husband and wife. They are permissible, because they are more than images. They are archetypes of man as the creature of God. We can avoid the term archetypes, as this term has a place in Jung's psychology, and we do better by distinguishing, as does Franz Rosenzweig, between 'image' (Hebrew: *temunah, pessel*), mirroring something between heaven and earth, on the one hand, and the prophetic word, parable, metaphor, *mashal,* on the other.

Only God is king. Only God is father. An earthly king or an earthly father is only in a limited way what 'our Father and King in heaven' is. The most perfect lovers do not rise in their yearning to that love with which God loves man; the most successful marriage does not bestow on man that fulfilled happiness of which Hosea's Zion speaks when she calls God 'My husband' (ii, 18). God, who appears as nothing when abstract thinking approaches Him, who appears as nothing when creative man wants to find Him in his own man-made works, has various attributes. Manifold are His *midot* (attributes) according to the *midrash,* the rabbinic exegesis. God is king. God is father. With these statements we do not transgress against the Second Commandment. They are the exposition of the Biblical prophets' experience of God which is accessible to every man.

The great contribution of the Jews to gentile history can best be understood by making a distinction between human creation and – as important as creation – synthesis. Maimonides wields his great influence on Europe through his influence on European scholasticism. Of his philosophy Julius Guttmann says in his standard work on the philosophy of Judaism that it is not original but based on the work of Islamic thinkers. But Guttmann adds: 'There is such a thing as originality of creative synthesis' (*Philosophies of Judaism,* The Jewish Publication Society of America, 1964, p. 153). The originality of creative synthesis of which Jews are capable always had its great hour when civilisation accepted the Jewish contribution. It happened at the end of the Islamic-Christian Middle Ages and also after the French Revolution. Between the end of the Middle Ages and the beginning of the Industrial Age the Jews made their contribution as bourgeois and as intellectuals towards justice, welfare and the civilised forms of life. Mankind needs the Jew. History as a gentile enterprise, as the enterprise of creative man, needs the Jew. The Jew, not bred by history, is what every man is: a creature of God. He is separated from the gentiles for one single mission: the worship of God in the midst of the world. Separation is the lot of the priest. Jews and Christians alike are separated from the gentiles. In each case it is a different separation, because sanctification and spiritualisation are two different ways.

THE CHRISTIAN BROTHERHOOD
OF THE SONS

Revolutions and wars not only devastate cities but also leave behind a fatherless generation. After the Great War a generation appeared on the scene which in its actions and beliefs could be characterised as fatherless. Before the Great War the feeling of being led by 'old men' depressed many minds aware of the shortcomings of the era. Just as during the Great War some said 'the British fight like lions, but are led by donkeys', in the years preceding the war the accusation was: 'The leaders are "old men" '. The age had filled its unruly sons with a belief, albeit utopian, in a better future. All this – the century before 1914 and the years of the two world wars – lies behind us. Both the faults of the 'old men' and the mistakes of the idealistic sons are past history. We are left with the sad experience that it is a bad time when fathers and sons do not 'walk together'. This phrase 'to walk together' which I had just written without any conscious intention of quoting a Biblical text, is from the Biblical passage about Abraham and Isaac: they 'walked together'. There is also Malachi's promise of a happy future in which God 'shall turn the heart of the fathers to the children and the heart of the children to their fathers' (iii, 24). This verse is often mentioned in sermons. What is too often left out is the verse which follows: 'Lest I come and smite the land with utter destruction.' Having seen cities devastated in Europe during two wars, having seen progress at the price of a world revolution which has not yet ended, we look to the antagonism of the generations, to the antagonism between fathers and sons, and ask 'can it be avoided?' To avoid this hard fact which dominates the natural life of the generations, we must enter into a religious enquiry.

What is there besides history? We have had two world wars and the cold war, and we ask 'is there no place where man has peace?' This question can be asked by the tired escapist. But it can also be the question of the God-seeker. He can be told: 'Eternity has no history.' (Franz Rosenzweig: *Stern der Erlösung,* III, 119). This sentence is self-evident to the Jew. It is not so to the Christian. As a Christian he knows of a point within history where eternity has broken into time, into history. He knows of an historical event where a second creation was added to the creation in the beginning, when a spiritual superstructure was laid upon creation. This happened, says the Christian, at the first Christmas.

With our statement, self-evident to the Jew, 'eternity has no history', the question arises, 'how do we Jews live our lives so that eternity resides in our midst?' God is eternal. How can living man come into the possession of the peace and holiness of eternal life? Rosenzweig writes: 'The Jew testifies his faith by begetting a son' (*Stern* III, 48). This is the nearest an English translation can approach to the telling pronouncement of the German original, in which the two words 'testify' and 'beget' sound nearly identical: (*zeugen – bezeugen*). What Rosenzweig means by this sentence is this: the Jew testifies his faith by marrying, raising a family and setting up a Jewish home. The table at which the family sit down for their meals is an altar. At this altar bread and wine are sanctified and grace is said. In his home, and not at all exclusively in history, the Jew meets God. In history, understood only as creations of state and culture, we do not find eternity. There we see man sacrificing himself to the many gods. History offers heroic ideals and spiritual views. The Jew does not trust the creations of history; he trusts God. 'The Jew trusts the blood' (*Stern* III, 50), not the spirit. This statement and that quoted above, 'the Jew testifies his faith by setting up a home and raising a family', must not be understood in the sense of racialism.

Rosenzweig wrote these two sentences in 1919 when he had no reason to guard his pen against a racialist misunderstanding. 'Blood' in Biblical semantics stands for universal characteristics. Man, every man is *bassar vedam,* flesh and blood. Man in his existence as creature of God, every man, not only a hero, not only a saint, can meet God. Therefore the prophet, as we saw (pp. 90–91), demands after the historical catastrophe of the destruction of the first Temple, that the Jewish people should not mortify itself, should not attempt to rise to a spiritual superstructure, but should remain on the human level. Rosenzweig does not quote Ezekiel's 'In thy blood live!'. His 'we alone trusted the blood' (*Stern* III, 49) has its power in its own originality. Rosenzweig, without being conscious of his verbal identity with Ezekiel, says exactly the same as Ezekiel. Ezekiel's 'In thy blood live' and Rosenzweig's 'We alone trusted the blood' rise from prophetic depth. Both Ezekiel and Rosenzweig alike point to the difference between Judaism and Christianity.

At the time of Ezekiel, Christianity was not yet at the side of Judaism. Rosenzweig's 'we alone' answers Christianity. It means: we Jews, not the Christians. They trust in the Holy Ghost, in the third person of the trinitarian God. 'We alone trusted the blood' means: only we Jews see every man and not only men of genius on the stage of history with the faculty of meeting God. Prophetic Judaism sees man speaking to God 'mouth to mouth'. What is needed for man's encounter with God is that trust which everyone experiences as a child in his father's house. Fathers and sons are engaged in history. It is each time a different engagement. In the household of God both fathers and sons have their mission. Today when the uprooted masses follow a father-figure, the return of the trust in a real father has to be acknowledged as necessary for the restoration of the health of private and public life.

In Genesis Chapter 22 we read of Abraham and Isaac on their way to an altar. We can read this chapter in close adherence to the narrative with its ancient background and yet discover something which refers to every man throughout the ages. It tells of a change which takes place when a youngster leaves adolescence and enters mature manhood. Noble youth is full of the desire to sacrifice itself. There is a cause. How else can youth serve the good cause than through readiness for sacrifice? Youth has no experience and no skill to serve mankind. But it has its life. To give their lives so that others may benefit is the desire of noble hearts. But there comes a moment which brings the understanding that the good cause can be served by hard work into which goes much sacrifice. But this sacrifice is without self-immolation. It is a sacrifice in which life is not sacrificed but which is rendered in obedience to demands as they appear in the course of life itself. When the understanding of this sacrifice arrives in the heart of a youth, he leaves adolescence behind and enters manhood. He ceases to be a 'son' and can become what a father is: a man obedient to the duties which have to be performed in life. Isaac's sacrifice is no longer what the noble heart demands. Isaac can leave the place where life is sacrificed. Isaac can grow up, marry and become what Abraham is: *a baal habayit,* the priestly father of a home. This is the story which happens eternally when history does not consume, as it so often does, the hecatombs of sacrifices and lets the young grow old. 'He was too young when he died,' says Nietzsche of Christ. 'Had he lived longer, his teaching would have become of a different kind.' He would have renounced what he had taught as a son who had not yet grown up to the stature of a father. Thus the Cross is the message of a sacrificed Isaac. Genesis 22 was changed in accordance with Christian teaching.

The three monotheistic religions differ in their concept of the father-son relationship. The Jew reads the story of Abraham and Isaac as an example of the union possible between father and son. The Mohammedan finds a short extract of the Old Testament story in his Koran. There the story is reduced to the commandment to Abraham: 'Sacrifice your son.' Abraham obeys. This unquestioning obedience to God is the faith of Abraham according to Mohammed. Fathers as lawgivers and sons obeying without a will of their own – this is Islam. The Christian reading of the story of Abraham and Isaac no longer sees the father in the centre. In the centre is the son. Father and son are different. The son has a role to perform which is not that of the father. There is the story of the One Son who is the son on the Cross, and there are the many sons in each generation. But as sons who are not yet fathers they are in their noble youthfulness prepared to follow the example of the One Son on the Cross.

The love of God is nowhere more profoundly experienced than in the knowledge that it is given to us unconditionally. No sacrifice is needed; without it man has received what is his life, his peace and his good portion. This knowledge is expressed in the words of the angel to Abraham: do not sacrifice your son. Genesis ch. 22 is the greatest gospel of love ever written. This gospel is to be found in the book which the Christians call the Old Testament. It is, therefore, a great mistake to utter the formula: Judaism is law, Christianity is love. The oneness of law and love is there in all the commandments of the Old Testament. The Jew, shaped by the Old Testament, or more correctly, not shaped by a civilisation but 'created by God' and left in his status as creature of God, moves easily from justice to love, from love to justice. The moral pagan, the Stoic, can reject the interference of love in the course of justice. The Christian sermon of love makes the profligate son forget that he has neglected the law which fathers teach their sons to obey. The Jew is free from the antinomy love – justice. The issue is not 'Jewish Law and Christian love', it is 'Islamic law and Christian love' (See the chapter 'Two Civilisations' in my *The Face of God after Auschwitz*).

The welcome to the profligate son in the story of Luke ch. 15 shows the love of the father for his unfaithful son. The son had turned away from his father's house, but returning in repentance he is received by his loving father. This story expresses in the form of a parable what the rabbinic saying formulates in the sentence: 'At a place where those who repent stand, not even the righteous are allowed to stand' (Talmud Berachot 34b). Luke's parable and the rabbinic formula show that both Judaism and Christianity reject a moral rigorism condemning sinners outright and finally. What the Jew will not accept and not even understand is the belief that it needs the way from sin to repentance – repentance understood as conversion – in order to meet God.

Through the act of conversion faith receives a liveliness which those who are without the momentary experience of conversion may often lack. Only where Jews live near Christians do they feel the need to raise their Jewish faith to doctrinal clarity. Jewish existence need not speak out in doctrines. Christian faith must speak in a thousand tongues; Christians must be guided by doctrine. The detour around sin makes converted man well fitted to formulate his faith, which appears as a new faith in a clear light. But to pursue righteousness and avoid the detour around sin is a great thing. Of an Islamic saint nothing else is said than that he was righteous and pious, whereas the Christian Church records in detail in the *acta sanctorum* those outstanding actions which justify the elevation of the saint above the righteous. But those who are neither saints nor sinners can live the good life. The Pharisees praise them, the Psalmist praises them, Islam praises them. The praise of the righteous will not cease to be sung by Jews in every generation. Christians may see those praised in such a decisive way as bourgeois types, respectable and no more.

The two theistic religions of Judaism and Christianity both have the love of God as their message and differ therein radically from the third theistic religion, Islam. Islam does not know of a loving God, nor of man resting in His love. Allah will become the God of the universe by an Islam spreading its doctrine all over the world – a conquering ideology will unify mankind – and man prepares the way for truth through his unrelenting action. The Arabic word 'Islam' does not mean the same as the Hebrew *shalom,* 'peace' – rest in the love of God; 'Islam' means 'submission' – to submit oneself to the fate which Allah decrees. Islam is an unceasing sequence of duties to be fulfilled. Compassion, the *rahma* which Mohammed ascribes to Allah, the *Mitleid* which Schopenhauer acknowledged as duty, is not love. Love flows from God to man and can flow from man to God. But a love which can only come from God but cannot be returned to God by man is not the love which the Old and New Testament preach, it is only *rahma,* only Mitleid (compassion). Schopenhauer thought he expounded Buddhist wisdom with his affirmation of compassion. He was mistaken. With his affirmation of compassion – a warm reaction of man to the suffering of his fellow-man – he is the champion of a humanism which, when entering politics, advocates the Welfare State, where man is supposed to be no longer in need of the love of his fellow-men.

That God chooses Israel not because of its greatness but because of its smallness, that God is the God of the weak, of the orphan, the widow, the stranger, is inconceivable to a Mohammedan, unless he is a Sufi, and as a Sufi he is under Christian influence. The Calvinistic belief that God is in the life of the successful is Mohammed's concept of the blessing of God. It is repugnant to Mohammed to assume that those who suffer are chosen. Admittedly, God has compassion on human frailty, but that God loves the weak more than the strong is inconceivable to Mohammed. He lacked the humility which alone could have taught him the Jewish-Christian concept of love. Certainly, Allah is to Mohammed the 'Much Forgiver', the *al-ghaffar,* which the *Shorter Encyclopaedia of Islam* translates as 'the forgiver *par métier.* But there is nothing in Islam which corresponds to Luke's parable of the profligate son and the rabbinic saying about the *baal teshuvah,* the returning sinner. The *baal teshuvah* does not consider himself as 'converted' but as a man who realises that he has strayed away from the right path, and who sees God as loving father forgiving the mistake (*shegagah*) of his children. It must also be remembered that Isaiah's 'The remnant shall return' means for this prophet

164

nothing else than disengagement from a wrong engagement in history, and a return to the creation in which history must retain its roots. The prophet pleads for a return to the world of the fathers. History can succeed as 'second creation', but only when anchored in the first Creation, which begins with the creation of heaven and earth and which blesses man with perfect sabbatical peace when fathers and sons are at one.

Having seen Judaism and Christianity in their difference from Islam but as near to each other, we can add a post-script in summary. To establish social life on the exclusive reign of love, even with the power of love to overrule justice, is impossible. The judge in a society which calls itself Christian has to condemn the accused where the law demands it. He cannot act as a Christian and put love above justice. The Church was only able to solve this dilemma by accepting the Old Testament at the side of the New Testament and declaring both Holy Scripture. In the course of the medieval Jewish-Christian dialogue – if a dialogue it was – the Church expressed its antagonism to Islam by identifying Judaism with Islam and by alleging: Judaism is the religion of law, Christianity the religion of love. The truth is that justice, love, compassion cannot be reduced to one doctrine in which they are united without contradiction.

The doctrine will always be involved in insoluble dialectics. But what is impossible to unite doctrinally can be united when man existentially follows justice, loves God and his neighbour and acts in compassion as a social being. Islam and Christianity are the triumphant doctrines of theism. Judaism is the 'seed' out of which grows the mighty tree with its two branches, Christianity and Islam. The Jew responds equally in his behaviour to the call of justice and the call of love, and he possesses the capacity of switching with lightning speed from justice to love, and from love to justice, always in harmony with the human situation and not bound by the rigid dictates of an institution. There is the Christian Church of love, there is the *Shari'a*, the written Law of the Mohammedan, but the Jew is the man who has retained the freedom to move in the quick decision of human reaction from justice to love and from love to justice.

Judah Hallevi's parable of the seed and the tree goes back to Isaiah's metaphor 'holy seed'. To give the word 'holy seed' a racial meaning is gross misunderstanding. True, it refers to the Jewish people. But it refers to it as a people whose faith allows it to remain in the state of the creature of God. Every man is born a creature of God. But history as shaped by Church and Islam can change the creature of God in accordance with the doctrines which these two theistic institutions propagate. But both Christianity and Islam will go astray where they cease to be what they are in healthy circumstances: the two branches of the tree grown from one seed, the holy seed of Judaism.

It is not 'law versus love', but faith of the fathers versus 'faith of the sons' which points the difference between Judaism and Christianity. Repentance, which both Luke and the rabbinic sentence quoted above equally praise, leads to a point where Judaism and Christianity no longer appear as equal forms of theism but reveal their difference. The Jewish commandment may be formulated as demanding: Repent and no longer do what is wrong! The Christian commandment is: Repent and believe! Conversion is repentance but one which leads to a new frame of mind. Conversion is what the Hellenistic word *metanoia* says: change of mind. For this Greek word no equivalent exists in the Hebrew Bible. Those who repent 'return'; those who are converted stand at the beginning. Conversion is a momentary experience of the soul, and with this experience, *the* Christian experience, the Christian is the eternal beginner. In each new situation of world history Christianity must begin anew with its mission of conversion. To begin is one thing, to shape one's whole life and the life of one's family over many years is another. The father is tested throughout his lifetime. The converted, on the other hand, stands at a new beginning. The spirit of this beginning has again and again to be recaptured. With this the Christian is eternally the son, starting new ways.

166

This is 'the eternal youth of Christianity' (Franz Rosenzweig) with its mission for the ever-changing scene of history. The Christian is always on his way, history does not stand still. The Jewish people has arrived. The children revive the faith of the fathers. The Jewish people has had its history. This history is closed, and we can always return to it. Eternity has no history. With eternity in our midst, it is the father who is in charge. With the duty of an eternally new beginning it is always the son who has his hour.

The sons bleeding in history, becoming rebels and patricides, the fathers becoming martyrs in the turmoil of history – can this curse be removed from history? This question can be answered by changing Malachi's text into a new version: I shall turn the hearts of the Jews to the hearts of the Christians and the hearts of the Christians to the hearts of the Jews. Even this new version would not suffice. The bourgeois is neither a Jew nor a Christian but is the remaining witness of the civilised pagan, the eternal Greek within the Christian world whom Islam has introduced into the theistic faith. The three theistic faiths, at peace with each other in spite of their differences, bring peace to mankind.

That no one comes to the Father except through the Son (John xiv, 6), is true for the Christian. It is not true for the Jew. The Jew does not 'believe', he trusts. He trusts that he encounters God – in life, in history and in life after death. Trust (*bitachon*) is a very simple thing, and a most difficult one. In trust man is bidden to 'walk humbly before God' (Micah, vi, 8). Trust has no reason, no proof, no basis on which it is founded. Trust rests on trust, it is a flame which burns by itself. Trust is not belief, because belief, Christian belief, rests on evidence, the evidence of an event in history. The 'Son' who leads to the 'Father' was born, suffered and died – a tale about a man who encountered God not as a family man, but as a young man and as one who changed history.

To change history is the eternal programme of the sons leaving their fathers' houses. To change history is a revolutionary act. The first to point to this eternal revolution which Christianity planted in the history of mankind, was Rosenzweig. His cousin, the historian Eugen Rosenstock-Huessy, made Rosenzweig's view his own in his work *On Revolution*. The first European revolution was the Papal revolution in the conflict about investiture: the Pope rose against the Emperor. The second revolution was Luther's Reformation, the third the Revolution in England, the fourth the French Revolution and the fifth, the Russian Revolution. Has the discovery of the atomic bomb in the course of the fifth revolution put an end to the unceasing wars of the human race, at least to world wars? Is progress no longer progress through sacrificial death? Has the time come for progress as conceived by the Jew, a progress which is possible without the sacrifice of the young Isaac?

Eugen Rosenstock-Huessy is no longer the only historian who sees the Christian element in the European revolutions. Friedrich Heer, Professor at Vienna University, sees 'Europe as the mother of revolutions' and writes a history of Europe as a history of sons perpetually rebelling against their fathers. The historian Toynbee with his formula of the 'aggressiveness' of the Christian has expressed, though in a muddled way, what the historians Rosenstock-Huessy and Heer describe with the clarity of exact research and what Rosenzweig formulated as a thinker. Rosenstock-Huessy is a Protestant baptised as a child by his Jewish parents. Friedrich Heer is a Roman Catholic belonging to the modernist wing of his Church. Both are historians with a genuine theological understanding of the periods of which they tell the tale. Toynbee, on the other hand, has his private theology to which he adds his undisciplined imagination.

Professor Heer sees the five European revolutions which Rosenstock-Huessy enumerates as a single one. He sees them as the consequence of the one great revolution which Augustine initiated. Augustine is the greatest disciple of Paul. Paul cut Christianity away from Judaism and so created the dichotomy of love and law. He did it to make Judaism, though in this changed form, available for the gentiles. Of Augustine Professor Heer writes: 'In him the eternally revolutionary, intellectual and spiritual mind and also the spirit of enlightenment were set free! (*Europäische Geistesgeschichte,* p. 29). Augustine according to Heer, created the Western world.

In his act of faith, in his conversion, the Christian is a beginner. Conversion is a revolutionary new beginning. Rosenzweig writes: 'The Christian is an eternal beginner, to finish is not his job, all is well that begins well. This is the eternal youth of the Christian.' (*Stern* III, p. 127). 'To finish' means to resort to law. Love can find fulfilment in the order of home and family and of social life. But such love enduring on every day level is not the Christian love which aspires to be more than the love which binds man and woman together and makes them one flesh. Law regulates the existing order. There is no Christian law, there is Christian love. Christian love sees the heaven open, sees the New Jerusalem. With his vision of a new order the Christian becomes the son who leaves his father's house. He becomes the youthful revolutionary. The world begins anew for him. The Christian is the son who assumes his own right. Prepared to leave father and mother, brother and sister, prepared to turn against them for the sake of his spiritual vision, the Christian is a Christian. While praising 'the eternal youth of the Christian' Rosenzweig remains a Jew. In Judaism fathers and sons are at one; they do not go different ways, 'they walk together' (Genesis ch. 22). In the rebellion of the sons against their fathers Rosenzweig sees not only the Christian but also the gentile factor. Rebellion as an entirely gentile event devoid of any Christian clemency is the experience of our time. The de-Christianised gentile is a pagan.

A Christianity uprooted from Judaism overlooked the paganism of the youth movements in Central Europe. The human community consists of various age groups: the young, the adults and the old. The community established by the German youth movement, the *Bund* (fraternity) united youth to a brotherhood consisting only of the young. Youth led by youth creates pagan society. The word *Führer* came from the ranks of the German *Wandervogel* which has nothing whatsoever to do with the Boy Scout Movement of the Anglo-Saxon countries. Two dates in the history of the German youth movement can sign-post the way which led from idealism to barbarism. The first date is spring 1912, when the meeting on the *Hohe Meissner* (a mountain in Thuringia) took place, the second is the 'first night' of Brecht's *Threepenny Opera,* October 28th, 1928. The meeting on the *Hohe Meissner* was, to all appearances, innocent enthusiasm. Life in itself was declared a fine thing, not in need of a code. What was needed were strong bodies and freedom from city-civilisation. There were many songs with an anti-bourgeois content, not much different from 'We shall overcome' or 'Little Boxes'. Songs with social revolutionary content, nationalistic and martial songs were all sung with equal fervour. The two German poets Stefan George and R. M. Rilke wrote poems which approved of the Youth Movement: Stefan George's

> *Wer je die Flamme umschritt,*
> *Bleibe der Flamme Trabant!*
> He who has once been a satellite of the flame
> Must forever remain faithful to the flame

was recited at the camp-fires. From this incantation the way led to the Horst Wessel song and to the oath sung by the S.S. 'Though all may become unfaithful, we remain faithful' – add: 'to the *Führer*'.

The 'first night' of Brecht's *Threepenny Opera* remains a date to remember. The nascent Nazi nihilism came to the fore on a Berlin stage. The idealists of the *Hohe Meissner* were now joined by types swayed by bitter cynicism and blind hatred. The young people, reports Willy Haas (*Literarische Welt,* Paul List Verlag, München pp. 144—149), applauded, stamped their feet, roared and rejoiced enthusiastically. After the 'Cannon song' the actors could hardly

carry on because the applauding audience threatened to storm
the stage. Were these youngsters communists or Nazis? Political cynics had become a united horde in that orgy with
its forebodings of the rebellion against mankind which started
in 1933. The patricides were ready for action. Of a generation like the applauding youngsters at Brecht's opera Simone
Weil said: 'Revolution is the opium of the people.' Haas,
the literary critic, an eye witness of the 'first night' performance, speaks of Brecht's 'affirmation of brutality and
rape, of his sadistic joy and his contempt for those who
became the victims of the rebellion.' It was an Englishman,
Leslie Paul, who in his writings analysed the German Youth
Movement and came to this conclusion: if western civilisation should collapse under the onslaught of barbarism, a
future historian would recognise the origin of this disaster
in the German Youth Movement. At the meeting on the
Hohe Meissner in 1912 romantics, sons of bourgeois homes,
enjoyed their ceremonial dancing round the camp fires, preferred instinct to reason and while flirting with tragedy and
death quoted Schiller's 'Life is not the most valuable of
possessions'. After the Brecht 'first-night', 'puerilism' – as
Huizinga diagnosed from neighbouring Holland – had taken
possession of a part of the German nation. The S.S. with
their slogan 'death is easy' appeared at the gates.

Owing to the deadlock in which Zionism saw the Jews
on the Continent with its growing antisemitism, the German
Youth Movement was adapted by Zionism to a Jewish Youth
Movement, preparing young Jews for the life in the agricultural settlements of Palestine. The Jewish Youth Movement led to the *kibbutz*. Martin Buber must take credit for
protecting the Jewish Youth Movement from what the German Youth Movement eventually became. Much has been
said and written about the *kibbutz*, and the controversy is
not yet resolved.

The century which witnessed the greatest tragedy of the
Jewish people with its six million martyrs murdered by the
Germans was also the century in which German Jews con-

tributed as much to mankind as did the Jews in the time of the Jewish-Arabic renaissance. There were philosophers of the stature of Hermann Cohen, Edmund Husserl and Franz Rosenzweig. Max Scheler, who was the son of a Jewish mother and grew up in the refined atmosphere of a Jewish bourgeois home, belongs to this group, as well as Simone Weil, Martin Buber and Freud. They all had no connection with that philosophy which led from post-Kantian idealism to the revolt of the young. They were shaped by their parental homes in which the 'God of the fathers' was worshipped. Most of all, it is Franz Kafka who restored the father to his place in human life. His *Letter to the Father,* never posted, is a gem among his writings and the best commentary on them. In his two novels *The Castle* and *The Trial* a profligate son endeavours to find his way back through the labyrinth of a 'time out of joint' to rightful authority, to the 'king', to the 'father'.

In the 'fraternity' (*Bund*) of the Youth Movement Judaism was better able to discover the point of departure from the rule ordained by the God of the Old Testament than was the Christian coming from the New Testament. The Old Testament commands 'Thou shalt love thy neighbour as thyself.' The New Testament, besides taking over this commandment from the Old, spiritualises the 'neighbour' into a 'brother'. In the brotherhood created by the Church those who are far away and those who are near are united in spirit. Under the rule of the Christian spirit there is no Jew or gentile, no Greek or barbarian, no master or slave. They are all brothers. As brotherhood the Church militant and triumphant is able to bring into her *oecumene,* into her Christian household, various nations, races, classes. The Christian Church is brotherhood; brotherhood is the Christian form of social life. This is the glory of the Church, and the Jew might be able to see this glory, whereas the Mohammedan is unable to do so. 'How good and how pleasant it is for brethren to dwell together in unity!' (Ps. cxxxiii, 1). Does the Psalmist refer to Christian brotherhood? This can-

172

not be the case, as Psalms, so different from Christian hymns, express the piety of the Old Testament with its commandment: 'Thou shalt love thy neighbour as thyself.' The difference between 'neighbour' and 'brother' can enlighten us about the difference between Jew and Christian.

The 'neighbour' of Leviticus, xix, 18 is the man next to you, that means every man; he is not what you are; he is different from you. You are you, and he is not you. But thou shalt love him, so that you can see him not as a he, standing outside, a man excluded from your fellowship, but as a man whom you can address as 'thou'. The commandment of the Old Testament establishes human fellowship, and human fellowship is different from Christian brotherhood.

Christian brotherhood can proclaim, 'There is no master and no slave.' Yet master remains master, and slave remains slave, they are brothers – in spirit. Spiritual brotherhood is not a small thing. But nor is fellowship which will not allow the distinction between master and slave to prevail. The American farmers often showed love for their negro-slaves, but they did not grant them justice, they refused their liberation. The American negro before the Civil War was as a Christian bound together in brotherhood with his master, but this brotherhood let him remain a slave. Kafka may have had the difference between brotherhood and fellowship in mind when he spoke of Christian coldness as different from Jewish warmth. Parents love their children, children their parents in the fellowship of flesh and blood. In Leviticus xix, 18, 'Love thy neighbour as thyself' means this fellowship of flesh and blood. The 'neighbour' is what you are, a creature of God, and therefore your brother, not only in spirit, but in the flesh. Christianity, with its mission to convert the gentiles, had, preaching spiritual brotherhood, an opportunity of de-nationalising the gentiles: in the Church there is no Jew and no gentile.

Nor is there father or mother, son or daughter (Matthew x, 37) in Christian brotherhood. Mozart had in his father a leader and mentor. There was a father-son relationship

173

in which the son owed much to the father. Mozart, as his *Magic Flute* testifies, believed in Freemasonry, which in his days still seemed to be identical with Johannine Christianity, a Christianity without the man-made institution of the Church. Mozart introduced his father into his lodge: his father became his brother. This transformation is deemed desirable and possible for the Christian. The father-son relationship in the flesh had often to be ignored in Christian politics, when sons said: one has to obey God more than one's father. Brotherhood as a spiritual relationship is necessary for a Church which preaches: Love your enemies! The Church says to warring gentiles: Fight, if fight you must, but remember, your enemy is your brother! The appeal to the spirit does not forge swords into ploughshares; the commandment 'love your neighbour as thyself', does. Brotherhood, as preached by the Church, did not stop the wars waged in Christendom. The fellowship of the creatures of God unites mankind. Brotherhood unites the sons who have risen against the fathers. The Christian heritage of patricide became apparent again in the modern chapter of the Christian nations. Democracy proclaiming *fraternité* began with regicide. The spirit praised as the creator begins its work by turning against Creation.

Pentecost is the Christian festival which commemorates the miracle of the spirit as recorded in Acts ii, 1–21. There Joel iii, 1–4 is quoted:

> *'And it shall come to pass afterward,*
> *That I will pour out My spirit upon all flesh;*
> *And your sons and your daughters shall prophesy,*
> *Your old men shall dream dreams,*
> *Your young men shall see visions;*
> *And also upon the servants and upon the handmaids*
> *In those days will I pour out My spirit . . .'*

So far Joel, the Jewish prophet. The wonderful poetry of his words must not draw our attention away from the sober reality of his expectations. Individuals, old men and

young men, servants, men and women will become endowed
with the prophetic gift. This gift does not raise human status
into spiritual status. The prophet is, according to the Jewish
understanding, not a superman but a man scrutinising contemporary history and private life for what is the will of God,
and acting in a way that this will be done. The Hebrew
word *nabi,* translated into the Greek word *prophetes,* 'carries
none of the meaning of "prophet" as one who is inspired,
who reveals – let alone predicts future events . . . If we still
insist on translating *nabi* as "prophet", we should each time
tell the unwary student that *nabi* is "prophet" *minus* everything that "prophet" means and connotes' (Edward Ullendorf
Thought Categories in the Hebrew Bible in *Studies in
Rationalism, Judaism and Universalism.* In Memory of Leon
Roth, Routledge and Kegan Paul, p. 285).

In Acts the spirit is the power which – as we hear
from the text – makes a disunited crowd of various nationalities a multitude speaking one single language; the spirit
creates a collective whole out of separated individuals; it
creates a Church. The spirit also creates the superhuman
faculty of geniuses and saints. The Jews, on the other hand,
as we read in the passage of the Acts, referred to above, say
of those whom the miraculous conversion of human nature
into spiritual nature has changed: 'They have been drinking'
(v. 13). Mohammedans, who not only reject but who, unlike
the Jews, have no understanding of the doctrine of the spirit,
are not allowed to drink wine. They also put decisive ob-
stacles in the way of the artist, who in his artistic creations
has rigidly to observe the commandment not to let anything
in heaven or on earth symbolise the unique majesty and
oneness of God.

How can the Christian concept of the spirit be reconciled
with monotheism? Can a Jew give an answer which acknowledges Christianity as a monotheistic faith? This is in
fact possible for him without relinquishing anything of his
Judaism. There is the one distinction holy-profane and the
other distinction spiritual-secular. A Jew knows what is spiri-

tual, just as a Christian knows what is holy. True, the words 'spiritual' and 'spirit', as the Christian understands them, do not occur in the Hebrew Bible (see my *Face of God after Auschwitz* pp. 166–7). Luke (ix, 3) changed the word *exodus,* meaning 'way towards freedom', into *exodos,* which means for him 'ascent away from life'. Spirit is 'ascent away from life'. Can a Jew understand the Christian uplift into the spirit? Anyone, even the Jew, listening for instance to Bach or to a folk-song, or reading a poem, or admiring a piece of art, will admit to being spiritually moved. This is an aesthetic experience. The Church as a spiritual institution makes full use of art. Christian art 'preaches' the Christian message. The spirit soaring to God remains connected with the same aesthetic valuation which man applies when he calls some-thing or somebody beautiful. Holiness, on the other hand, is connected with ethical valuation. The life characterised by holiness is inseparably connected with morality. The difference between Jew and Christian is not that the first understands only what is holy, the latter only what is spiritual. The difference is that Jewish life is *constituted* through the distinction holy-profane, Christian life through the distinction spiritual-secular. The Christian Church, as a spiritual institu-tion, is a brotherhood. The Jew is a member of a holy fellowship. 'Holy' in Hebrew means 'separated'.

The Christian Church, a brotherhood, is bidden to go out into the world and to devalue the gentile world of the fathers and to make the gentiles sons of a Father who is their father not in the blood but in the spirit. The Christian brotherhood turns to Asia to bring a new son to the father: the Buddhist. Ninian Smart and Arnold Toynbee are playing with fire when they think Buddhism can be used to give new strength to Christianity. Here the Jew Franz Rosenzweig, speaking of 'the eternal youth of Christianity', has a truer approach. A Jew can remain a Jew and still approve of the mission of Christianity. It is a mission to turn gentiles into Christians. It cannot be a mission to turn Jews into Christians, because everything the Christian has, comes to him from the

Jew. Spirit becomes a mere ghost, a nebulous apparition of the imagination, unless rooted in and connected with the understanding of what is holy.

The gentile who is converted to Christianity joins the spiritual community of the Christian Church. The gentile who becomes a 'proselyte of righteousness' welcomed into the House of Israel leaves his nation. Holiness means separation. Can one leave one's nation? The Christian remains the national he was before his conversion. His entry into the spiritual brotherhood of the Church does not put an end to his national status. A gentile who becomes a Jew not only leaves his nation, he leaves the community of all nations. This is difficult. It is difficult for the Jews themselves, backsliding Jews always want 'to be like the gentiles'. The word holy in the meaning of separated creates a difference which is radical and leaves the important dilemma belief – unbelief behind.

A rabbinic homily tells the story that God offered 'Sinai' to all nations. Nobody wanted it. Even the Jewish people did not want it. So God took Mount Sinai and thrust it upon the Jewish people, so that it could not escape. It had to become the Jewish people. It became the Jewish people not through a creed which it would have confessed as the Christians confess their creed. The Jewish people became what it is through an act of God, the Creator of heaven and earth. With this understanding the question of welcoming proselytes is taken out of our human hands. It is left to God to work out how gentiles are able to join the House of Israel. The rabbinic legislation for the Jewish status of the 'proselyte of righteousness' follows God's providence. It must not precede it.

Who wants to become a Jew, though? More than a hundred years before Auschwitz, Heine wrote (in *Shakespeare's Women*): 'What martyrdom have the Jews suffered because of this idea (monotheism)! And what greater martyrdom is still ahead of them? I shudder at the thought of it and boundless compassion touches my heart.' Reviewing the history of

Jewish martyrdom in the Middle Ages, Heine thinks that in those centuries Judaism was different from Christian and Mohammedan monotheism 'only through different interpretation'. In his own time, Heine says, the situation threatens to be more dangerous. 'Should Satan, i.e. sinful pantheism, win, (with the word 'pantheism' Heine summarises the whole German post-Kantian philosophy) – may all the saints of the Old and New Testaments and the Koran protect us from this victory! – a storm of persecution will break on the heads of the poor Jews which will surpass all their former sufferings!'

Who wants to be a Jew? We now ask the question no longer to solve the difficult rabbinic dilemma concerning the welcoming of proselytes into the Jewish fold, we ask it on behalf of the whole Jewish people. The answer may be found in the lives of the Biblical prophets. Which of them wanted to be a prophet? The answer is: none. But they served in their holy mission and served well, an example for future generations. Holy means separated. The coal which purifies the lips of Isaiah reminds of the suffering of being singled out. Is the Jewish people a community believing in God? What would statisticians have to say about this question? The Jewish people has a relationship with God even more important than the one established through belief. With belief un-belief entered the history of man. Every Christian knows that. He knows the text: 'I believe, O Lord, help Thou my unbelief!' Jews who want to remain Jews after what happened in Auschwitz are truly Jews. The Jewish people has always been a people of survivors. They do not want to give up the privilege of belonging to the 'remnant'; they want to belong to the persecuted rather than to the persecutors. The Jewish people, walking in 'the burning fiery furnace' of history and remaining unhurt like Daniel and his friends, are surrounded by the miracle of God acting through the Jewish people in the history of the gentiles.

The Jewish people, the separated people, therefore the holy people, is a God-made people. In our nobility and in our shabbiness, in our cultural refinement and in our vulgarity, in our endurance and in our weakness, in our glory and in the shame of our de-humanisation in Auschwitz – we are the people of God; a people not merely of believers in God – that we are too – but a people in whom everyone, Jew himself and gentile alike, meets his father in heaven who 'will swallow up death for ever; ... And the shame of His people will He take away from off all the earth' (Isaiah xxv, 8). We did not choose to be Jews, God has chosen us.

Jews who are faithful remain Jews. 'To be faithful' is in Biblical Hebrew *ha-ameen,* which Christian translators render 'to believe'. Jews and Christians believe in God. But the truly Jewish word which corresponds to the Christian 'belief' is 'trust'. In trust is everything. Paul writes: 'There are three things which last for ever: faith, hope and love. But the greatest of them all is love' (I Cor. xiii, 13). The sentence 'the greatest of them all is love' adds nothing to the preceding sentence, in which love is already mentioned. A Jewish formulation, suggested by Franz Rosenzweig at the end of his *Stern der Erlösung,* would read: 'The greatest thing is trust. From it can grow faith, hope and love.' The Jewish formulation, which enumerates what grows from the seed of trust, stresses a point which Christians should never forget but alas have forgotten so often: Christianity is true Christianity when it retains its roots in Judaism.

ISLAMIC SUBMISSION TO THE LAW

At the centre of Gotthold Ephraim Lessing's play *Nathan the Wise* stands the parable of the three rings. By means of this parable Lessing explains his attitude towards the three monotheistic religions – Judaism, Christianity and Islam. A father has three sons. In his possession is a precious ring. To which son is he to bequeath it? He loves his three sons equally. He finds a way out of the dilemma by asking a goldsmith to make two other rings in such a way that no human eye shall be able to discern any difference between the three rings. When the father died each of the sons inherited a ring and each could claim that his was the genuine one. The moral of the parable is that the question 'who possesses the genuine ring?' cannot be answered. But Lessing adds a postscript. It is only at the end of days that it will be known just what the whole truth is; and in the interim man, be he Jew, Christian or Muslim, must live according to what he believes is the truth and, by his good deeds, must try to prove that he is on the right road. This means that he has no theoretical proof for the truth of his religion, but that he does have the practical solution of making it apparent that his life is guided throughout by the truth of God.

Lessing's parable of the three rings advocates an open society. The Middle Ages had their period in which an open society existed. The reign of the Emperor Frederick II was one of those periods. At his famous court in Sicily Jewish, Christian and Islamic scholars discussed their philosophical, political and theological problems. With the death of Frederick II in 1250, everything changed. Historians compare the year 1250 with the year 1914: 'The lights went out all over Europe'. The creative forces of the High Middle Ages

180

came to a halt. Christendom and Islam no longer penetrated each other beneficially. From the thirteenth century to the nineteenth century Islam was in a state of stagnation: for the *shari'a* innovation meant heresy, deadly sin. In the Christian West it was not much different: *reformatio* and *renovatio* did not mean progress but return to the sacred old order. Everything had to remain according to the old principles. The Middle Ages which had become decadent speak out in the Encyclical of Pope Pius IX (*Quanta cura* 8.12.1864) which refers to the revolution of 1848 with utter condemnation. 'Revolution is the inspiration of the devil, it aims to destroy Christianity and build paganism on its ruins.'

The impact of Islamic civilisation on Christianity was considerable and was made possible through the great mobility of Mediterranean man. Pilgrims, scholars, crusaders and Jews travelled on the roads and connected North and South, East and West. The Jewish ghetto was not yet a prison but was still a home. The Mediterranean Jew, as physician, as translator from Arabic into Latin, and as trader connected provincials with the intellectual climate of the world. *Ubique sunt Hebraei* (everywhere there are Jews) reports a chronicler of the early thirteenth century.

The twelfth century was the age of the religious disputations. Heinrich Heine, in his charming poem *Disputation* is sarcastic about the religious value of such meetings and he mocks them as tournaments of clerics. Above all, 'rabbi and monk' are both not to his taste. Heine has, in this case at least, the approach of a Liberal to whom the Middle Ages means nothing but a dark age. Lessing's parable recaptures the seriousness of the medieval discussion between Jew, Christian and Muslim. Europe was open to Islam, Islam to Christianity, and the Jew lived in both, in the Christian and the Islamic world. This co-existence of Jew, Christian and Muslim did not necessarily create the cynicism of which the story of the 'three great deceivers', i.e. Moses, Jesus and Mohammed, is proof. Mohammed has been accused of be-

ing, partly at least, responsible for this story. He calls the
Old Testament the New Testament and the Koran the three
successive forms of revelation. This robs each of them of
its unique truth and makes Moses, Jesus and Mohammed
as human vehicles of revelation equally lacking undisputed
authority. From here it is only one step to the cynical story
of the 'three great deceivers'. Lessing's parable recalls the
seriousness and the creative possibilities of the dialogue between the three monotheistic religions. Islam preserves the
spirit of antiquity. Our present civilisation is not only a
Judaeo-Christian civilisation but has a third element: the
Graeco-Roman element. Islam points to this element.

A religious dialogue is not an exercise in comparative
religion. Where the Jewish-Christian dialogue sinks to the
level of an intellectual duel without commitment, cynicism
will creep in, as it does in the transformation of the parable
of the three rings into the story of the 'three great deceivers'.
Lessing's parable points to a possibility for our own future.
In the dialogue between Jew, Christian and Muslim a new
search for God can come to life. If this dialogue is not a
search for God but has the hidden aim of conversion by
intellectual means, the scepticism of Heine's poem is justified.
The dialogue of the members of the monotheistic family is
an undertaking comparable to worship, from which it is
different. (Jew, Christian and Muslim can attend respectfully
and even devoutly their respective divine services but cannot
give up the differences between Jewish, Christian and Islamic
divine service.)

For Franz Rosenzweig there are not three, but only two
ways of testifying to the one truth – the way of Judaism and
the way of Christianity. Rosenzweig will not acknowledge
Islam as a monotheistic religion. To him, Islam is a religion
of reason and duty, and it is without revelation.
Rosenzweig was unfair to Islam, precisely like many Christian
theologians who have seen it as Semitic Hellenism or as
a Christian heresy. Mohammed has been called the greatest
plagiarist of world history. More to the point is Karl Becker,

a German Islamist who has called Islam a carrier of religions. Indeed, the Jewish and Christian elements in Islam cannot be overlooked. An attack on Islam is therefore often a boomerang which rebounds on Judaism or Christianity.

Rosenzweig's misconception of Islam has consequences for his own understanding of Judaism. The Jewish people has lived for centuries, indeed up to the present day, under the influence of Islamic civilisation. In the Middle Ages, the Jewish people had, in its own cultural set-up, an Islamic way of life. Rosenzweig defends such forms of communal life as Jewish, although they have their origin in Islam. When he writes 'you can run away from the Law, but you cannot change it', he is not aware that what he is saying could well be a quotation from the *Shari'a*. Since Mohammed is regarded as the last of the prophets, prophecy as the continuous force of criticism and free enquiry is excluded from religious life, which is only accorded recognition in its character of unchanged tradition. Rosenzweig's dictum about Jewish Law just quoted obliterates the difference between the Jewish and the Islamic doctrine of Law. Rosenzweig, who wished to be thought of as a liberal Jew, becomes rather the advocate of a Jewish *status quo* and the defender of the Jewish Middle Ages – a thinker who, it is now even alleged, stands on the side of orthodox Jewish obscurantism.

The second consequence of this error regarding Islam is of wider relevance. The Christian theologian who does not understand Islam is not able to make sense of the European class founded on reason and law. That class, standing in the midst of Christendom but never acknowledged by Christian doctrine, was the *bourgeoisie*. A Christian rehabilitation of bourgeois life has never been forthcoming. The very word 'bourgeois' has a derogatory meaning. Whereas in France the *citoyen* has the halo of citizen-soldier and patriot, the French *bourgeois* is without such glory; he represents nothing more than good living. In Germany the word *Bürger*, although imbued with respectability, carries the stigma of inferiority engendered through not belonging to the aristocracy. Above all, if a Christian becomes a bourgeois he ceases to be a Christian. Why? The world of today is divided into two halves, one of which is called the bourgeois West. Is the West, then, in so far as it is bourgeois, not Christian?

Lessing's parable sees the three monotheistic religions as equals, but it does not draw any distinctions between them. But their equality need not be understood as identity; as between themselves they are different. Their difference becomes clear when we look at the Jewish, Christian and Mohammedan exegeses of Genesis 22. The great message of this chapter, according to the Jewish understanding of it, consists in exactly what the text says. God does not want Isaac to be sacrificed. God's love and mercy are available for man without having to be earned by sacrifice. Isaac returns home, marries, and himself becomes a father. That is the story of Abraham – a story dubbed by Kierkegaard a bourgeois idyll. But is it possible for God to be revealed in greater glory than as giving us life although we have done nothing to deserve it?

The Christian exegesis of Genesis ch. 22 changes the story. Isaac is sacrificed. Some one has to suffer and die, in order that man may live and be happy. Love is sacrificial love. The Koran has but a short extract of the story. Abraham is bidden 'sacrifice your son', and he obeys. That is all. The faith of the Muslim is the submission of his will to the will of God. He turns to God with a radical 'Thy will be done', and his obedience is his faith.

This threefold exegesis, although each motif is different, does not make it possible to say which one is more profound than the other two. We come back to Lessing's parable, with its emphasis on the undistinguishable equality of the three religions. Even though it is not possible to call any one of the three 'higher' or 'lower' than the others, their difference is apparent and must be carefully investigated.

It was a Christian mystic, Angelus Silesius (1624–77), who transplanted the threefold form of the foregoing exe-

184

gesis into the heart of Christianity itself. Just as we distinguish between Judaism, Christianity and Islam, so he saw three different forms within Christianity itself, explaining the doctrine of the Trinity not as three static ideas, but as referring to a process within the history of mankind.

> *First was the Father, now is the Son:*
> *The Spirit will be here on earth on*
> *the day of glory.*

Accordingly Schelling – and after him Rosenzweig – distinguished between the Petrine Church in the era of the Catholic Middle Ages and the Pauline Church which begins with the Protestant Reformation and lasts until the French Revolution. The Church which then enters history is the Johannine Church which is nowadays superseding the Constantinian Church. The Petrine Church, that is to say the Constantinian Church, uses law combined with power to sanctify human order, it is a denominational imperialism: the church militant aspires to make all infidels into believers. The Pauline Church, on the other hand, christens the human soul; it converts the poet within man, transforming the ever-changing imagination into an ever-identical faith, into 'faith alone'. But with its 'naught but faith' this Church lets the world slip away, and the Johannine Church has to take over. The Johannine Church likewise christens man, but the whole of man and not only his soul; man, endowed with body and soul and living his life in society, is summoned to become a Christian of the non-political, spiritual pattern.

How can Judaism fit into this philosophy of history? Here we have to set another parable at the side of Lessing's parable of the three rings and Angelus Silesius' vision of the three Churches. It is the parable of Judah Hallevi about the seed and the tree. He saw Christianity and Islam not as new religions but as monotheistic civilisations, as one tree with two mighty branches growing from a common seed. That seed is Judaism.

Judah Hallevi's parable of the seed and the tree with its

two branches puts Christianity and Islam, those two differing forms of monotheism, on an equal level. That equality consists in a fact which, although overlooked up till now, is nevertheless clearly visible in the two thousand years of Christian and fourteen hundred of Islamic history. Both Christianity and Islam created their own respective cultures and civilisations. The history of the West represents, for all to see, two civilisations – one Christian and one Islamic. Islam belongs to the West. The dialectic between love and law can be resolved neither within a single institution nor within a single civilisation. The civilisation of the West is based upon the two monotheistic civilisations, Christianity and Islam. To speak of 'Jewish culture', or (the same thing) a 'Jewish civilisation' is a misconception. In so far as Judaism holds fast to its prophetic element, it is debarred from the possibility of fulfilling itself in the sort of creativity that establishes states, cultures and civilisations. What is Jewish about the so-called 'Jewish intellectual'? With his uprootedness from reality, he has his habitat in the spiritual and intellectual sphere created by the Christian division between spirit and flesh, soul and body. What is Jewish about the so-called 'Jewish bourgeois'? With his trust in reason, and his submission to the moral law, he has his habitat in a sphere which is a colony of Islam planted in the midst of the Western world.

Everyone agrees that the bourgeois era began with the French Revolution. When Shelley wrote a poem about it he gave it the title *The Revolt of Islam*. He castigates the zealotry of the demagogues, but does not disapprove of the aim of the Revolution itself, and can write 'the sympathies connected with that event extended to every bosom'. The words are quoted from the preface to his poem. Like others of his contemporaries, he found Islam more natural and more human than Christianity. Islam rejected a dualism that would exalt the soul above the body. Islam keeps faith with man, who is permitted to remain a whole man. At the same time as Shelley was calling the French Revolution the revolt of

Islam, Goethe was writing his *West-östlicher Divan*. With the French Revolution there begins, according to Schelling and Rosenzweig, the Johannine era – a Christianity without dogma and, unlike Petrine Christianity, without a Christian law. In the present, Johannine, epoch intellectual and bourgeois become visible entities, and at long last justify themselves in the sense of finding their rightful place within a monotheistic civilisation. To move on from this point of our religio-sociological analysis, and to speak of a *Jewish* intellectual or of a *Jewish* bourgeois, involves us in an enquiry of some importance. In what way, we must ask, has Judaism been the leaven that has changed in the one case a Christian and in the other an Islamic character to such a degree that the attribute *Jewish* can be at all apposite?

That which appears, in institution and civilisation, as love and law in counterpoised opposition, as the contrast of mercy and justice, can live side by side within the man who is not shaped by civilisation but retains his human wholeness. No institution, no civilisation, no achievement of creative man can have the attribute 'Jewish'. There exists, of course, the Hebrew word *avodah*, which has a double meaning. It comprises two actions which are elsewhere generally thought of as contradictory to each other. *Avodah* means both *work* and *worship,* worship of God and ordinary work, the work which man must needs perform in order to maintain himself. Promethean man – every creative man, that is – knows of a third activity; self-fulfilment in art and in politics, in culture and in civilisation. Christianity aligned art with worship and built the Church alongside the State. Christian civilisaton is a superstructure built by Promethean man who has been christened. Marx condemned the Christian superstructure as a betrayal of the material world: and so did Islam. Islam turned aside from spiritual holiness, and worshipped instead terrestrial holiness: the world itself is the creation of God. Man can of himself, without any change effected by an inner conversion, turn to God.

Islam never came into contact with a policy in which

man is free. Islamic Hellenism never encountered Athenian democracy, but only the tyranny of disappearing antiquity. It was not the state, but private society and the family that were sanctified by the *Shari'a*, the holy Law of Islam. Religion and Law became identical. Nothing whatsoever of the social and material world was to be excluded from sanctification through the legal supervision of the *Shari'a*, the Islamic legal code. But nor was the material world itself intended to be raised to a spiritual level. Why should it be? 'The substance of the matter is obedience', said Simone Weil. That is, indeed, a statement begotten of piety, albeit not of Christian piety. Christianity and Islam, so close to each other because of their common origin in Judaism, are, as civilisations, divided by an unbridgeable gulf. The Jewish people had its history within Christian and Islamic civilisations and yet remained different from both of them. Seen from the standpoint of the Hebrew word *avodah,* the work-and-worship enjoined upon the Jew, Christian civilisation is but spiritual super-structure. What did the Jew contribute, then, to these two civilisations? He gave himself, and in so doing gave humanity. The Jew, as the word *avodah* implies, has no mission other than to work and pray. He must be a *Mensch* – he must be human. It is man's humanity which can combine love and law, mercy and justice. But in Christianity, love supreme, and in Islam, Law supreme, constitute civilisations that are different from each other.

In our own nuclear age, which has put all established civilisations into a state of crisis, it is a consoling thought that man need not be identified with his own civilisation. Aloof from that civilisation, he is at once in the situation in which every Biblical prophet found himself. The prophet was taken apart from the multitude, and had the task of telling others that in the destruction of the Temple not God, but man had suffered defeat. The work of man's hand, a civilisation, was being thrown into the melting-pot. The very word 'religion' has become discredited for many people, because it represents a civilisation in which a monotheistic religion appeared on the stage of past history. Bonhoeffer demands a 'religionless Christianity'. Rosenzweig states, with satisfaction, that in the whole of his substantial work *Der Stern der Erlösung* the word 'religion' does not occur once. Both Bonhoeffer and Rosenzweig are expressing what Schelling, with reference to Angelus Silesius, called the 'Johannine age'. Of these three witnesses of the coming age, which has already begun, two are Protestants and one is a Jew. They are joined by Professor Heer, himself a Catholic historian. Heer demands that conversion should not be the first thought in the mind of a Christian when he meets a non-Christian. Rather, it should be his task to give himself to his fellow-man as a Christian personality (*Offener Humanismus* p. 359). Jew, Christian and Muslim can enter into a true dialogue because they have to express what they stand for in their personal existence, and because they are no longer represented by a Jewish, Christian or Islamic civilisation styled the Jewish, Christian or Islamic 'religion'. The Jew has always been a human type. This now applies equally to the Christian and the Muslim because the two monotheistic civilisations which they represented so mightily in the Middle Ages no longer have any impact upon the world. The world today is divided into the democratic West and the communist East, and neither of the two can be fittingly identified with either Christianity or Islam. Both Christian and Muslim have entered a new era since the French Revolution. Progress has taken place: to put it in the words of Bonhoeffer, 'the world has come of age', or, to use the terminology of Angelus Silesius, 'the Johannine age is here'. Neither the Church nor the *Shari'a* makes our new age. It is neither a Christian civilisation in the West, nor an Islamic one in the East, that dominates our modern world. The world is one. East and West have met, and the world will be shaped anew through three types, the Christian, the Muslim and the Jew. In Christianity the sacrificial love of sons offering themselves for others, in Islam obedient submission to the authority of the fathers, and in Judaism the happiness

189

in which fathers and sons are united – here is a trinity in which Christian, Muslim and Jew can co-operate, and can collectively enter into a dialogue with a party that has never, hitherto, belonged to their own family: the Buddhist. Prophetic Judaism is needed to contradict Buddhism. Asia wants, and is indeed entitled to retain her own civilisation. That circumstance will itself prevent Christian or Islamic civilisation from penetrating Asia. But to the Christian and Muslim who come to her as Christian and Muslim persons, Asia is wide open. And where the Christian and the Muslim can live, the Jew can also live.

There is no disintegration here, amounting to an end; but rather a regrouping. Medieval Christianity and medieval Islam break up, and a Jewish, a Christian, and a Muslim form of personal existence are set free. The 'Johannine age', the Christianity without law and dogma which Schelling and Rosenzweig saw as entering our life after the French Revolution, does not involve the abolition of what Petrine and Pauline civilisation, the Christianities of law and dogma, have contributed. What is truly new does not destroy the old, but revives it. Freemasonry misinterprets the Johannine age as being disrupted from the past. The well-known nineteenth-century Viennese preacher, Dr A. Jellinek, was influenced by this misinterpretation when he said, 'Judaism is now called upon to build on the ruins of religions its Third Temple, of the true religion.' The Austrian rabbi, in the days of that virulent antisemitism which preceded Hitlerism, could place no hope in the Church which he observed participating in antisemitism. Probably unknowingly, he was preaching Freemasonry and not Judaism. Lessing was interested in the Freemasons but never joined them. It seems that in the days of classical Enlightenment Freemasonry was not yet what it is today – a travesty of monotheistic religion. The Johannine age of which Schelling and Rosenzweig hopefully spoke does not rest upon the 'ruins' of the two preceding ages. In the regrouping that takes place intellectual and bourgeois come forward anew, as far as their manifest presence on the scene is concerned: but they were in fact born and bred in the preceding Christian-Islamic civilisation.

Beside the intellectual and the bourgeois there stands the soldier. War as a crusade, as the 'holy war' of the Muslim, did not end with the Christian and Islamic Middle Ages; it merely transformed national wars into 'zoological' wars. Among the types of human character to which our civilisation has given birth the soldier must not be forgotten. Citizen-soldiers of the two world wars suffered as did those who died in Auschwitz. We may observe these soldiers in their obedience to authority – the great virtue of the Muslim. We must also view them in the setting of the sacrifice in which they died so that others might live. The tomb of the Unknown Warrior revives the symbol of the Cross; no one can pass a war memorial without being reminded of the Golgotha of our own time. The inhumanity of Auschwitz began with the inhumanity of the trench warfare of 1914–18. The youth that died in Flanders died in its own Auschwitz. The genocide of Auschwitz began in Verdun, which a German general called his blood-pump; and the French commander who opposed him was no less limited mentally in allowing himself to accept a method of fighting which made genocide an instrument of war.*

The two thousand years of Christianity have been two thousand years of war. The 'Holy War' which Mohammed taught the Muslim to fight was a Christian conception. In the China of Confucius the soldier has no status – he is on a par with the brigand. In Christendom it is different: here the principle of 'Render unto Caesar the things which are Caesar's' is no less important than is the second half of the verse. It is a principle which makes of the soldier who sheds his own blood for his country a Christian figure; and it makes the state, though it be different from the Church, its equal. The state is a secular institution, but a secular institu-

---

* The last sentences of this paragraph must not be taken out of the context of this book. What the Germans did to the Jews was a unique criminal act without parallel in the history of mankind.

tion that exists because the Church exists. The secular realm stands bathed in the light that proceeds from the Church. The secular element in it itself has its origin in the Church. Buddhist civilisation is not secular in the way that Christian civilisation is: Buddhist civilisation is Buddhist – not secular.

Buddhist civilisation has no concept of history, and presupposes a reality which is not yet purged of gods and spirits as is Western civilisation. Asian 'reality' is like a dreamland, as we see it in the drawings of Japanese and Chinese artists. In the tender lines and flourishes of these drawings, neither trees, stones, mountains, rivers nor the human figures among them have any contours. They have no existence of their own, but flow into each other to make up something which is really nothing at all, like the hub in the middle of a wheel. A wheel cannot be imagined without a hub, but the hub is merely the nothing without which the spokes of a wheel could not exist. In the Buddhist cosmos, sustained by the nothing as the spokes of the wheel are sustained by the hub, things and living beings are nothing in themselves; actions do not have a real purpose, everything is according to an aesthetically strict form, and everything in the social sphere is conduct and etiquette without moral justification. No one ought to cry out against cruelty perpetrated upon himself or upon others. Pain is unredeemable: and it has to be borne without reproach and bitterness. One cannot, here, love one's neighbour in the way in which the Hebrew Bible bids us love him, because one's neighbour is not discovered as a neighbour. Your fellow man is not 'like you', as the Bible says of one's neighbour; he is *tat tvam asi* – identical with you, even as a grain of sand in a heap is identical with other grains of sand. It is this world about which the Mona Lisa smiles with an expression so successfully caught by Leonardo da Vinci: it is a cold, impassive smile, outwardly friendly, but in truth cruel. It is the smile of the Buddha. Westerners, too, can of course learn to smile like that: but the moment that smile steals over their faces they cease to be Westerners. How near to each other, Judaism, Christianity, and Islam are when viewed from the background of Buddhist civilisation – because there is in it nothing at all of Judaism, Christianity, or Islam. Buddhist civilisation is Asia: Europe, Western civilisation, is of Jewish, Christian and Islamic make.

Rosenzweig is aware of the Christian element in the secular civilisation of the West. In his youth, when he first encountered Zionism, he was afraid that a Jewish state might transform Jews into Jewish Christians. (It is rumoured that the Vatican cherishes as a hope what Rosenzweig perceived as a danger.) The Christian mission to Jewry has never had the slightest effect on the Jews. But a situation can arise – as it did arise in the early Church – in which Christianity grows out of Judaism. Christianity always grows out of Judaism: that is the glory of the Jew. The Hebrew Bible in the hands of Christians, the *opiniones judaicae* adopted by Gentiles create Christianity. Whether Jews are present in the flesh or not, Judaism is an element in Western civilisation. A further probability arises when the Jew, deeming himself to be a faithful Jew, becomes in thought and action a Christian. Rosenzweig, realising that the state as a secular institution is still under the influence of the Church, pondered about a Jewish future in a Jewish state. Just as the Church is a state transformed by Judaism, so might not a Jewish state transform Judaism into elements of which one – the necessary spiritual opposition to power – becomes a Christian element?

In the Hebrew Bible the message for the servant of the Lord is a message for priest, teacher, preacher or prophet. It is the call to be ready for martyrdom. The soldier has the message of the Cross; in both instances it remains a message to the effect that someone must die in order that others may live. In the soldier's case the martyr's death is offered to a hero who no longer, like the Greek hero, dies for his own glory, but who dies for the glory of God. The message of the Cross makes of the soldier a Christian figure. The Jew of the Diaspora fought in two world wars and yet remained a Jew. A dilemma now begins to face the Jew who thinks about Judaism. The Jew who, with his own State of Israel, has now entered the realm of the *polis*, faces something of which he is morally bound to take cognisance: the rise of a tension between teaching and governing, between persuasion and the application of power, between spiritual and temporal power. In Jewish existence – in the private existence of any person – such dualism does not come to the fore. As citizens of the Jewish state Jews will therefore be able, step by step only, and in continuous watchfulness, to preserve their own Jewish existence.

The Christian controversy between State and Church is today reappearing in Israeli affairs. In her forthcoming and unavoidable *Kulturkampf* Israel will have to learn from Church history how, in the European Middle Ages, the struggle between Church and State made Western civilisation a fortress of the freedom of man. Christianity has also to be duly appraised for its faculty of paving the way for technological civilisation. The Jewish doctrine of creation, taken over into Islamic teaching, sees the world as 'very good' (Genesis i, 31) and leaves man, as the creature of God, with his human status unchanged. Christian doctrine sees the world as not yet redeemed on its first day and as remaining unredeemed *ante Christum natum*. The Christian division between creation and redemption – redemption being the cosmic correction of creation – between flesh and spirit, can tell of a world which is material, neutral or even wicked, and at the silent disposal of man. The Christian view of man's status made it possible for him to become the subtle workman – technological man who applies to his work one side only of his human existence, his mental faculties. Adam works on the land with his physical strength; but technological man is no longer Adam. He is 'second Adam'. He is man shaped by the division between spirit and flesh. The progress of technological civilisation has been bought at a price. Man has lost his wholeness – a unity undivided into spirit and flesh; and the world has lost its glory which the Psalmist praises and has become instead but neutral matter.

Man, the priestly father of his family – negatively assessed by Christianity as the bourgeois but sedulously safeguarded by the Law of the Torah and by the *Shari'a,* the Law of Islam – is threatened with being edged out of the realm of technological civilisation altogether.

The Islamic countries realise perfectly well that they have to pay for their westernisation. The West has freedom. But Islam has equality, a brotherhood not compromised by any Christian division between the highly specialised scientist or technician on the one hand and, on the other, the masses who are to become cogs in a vast machine-civilisation. Islam was once capable of affording a dignity to the man of the Hellenistic mass-age, and it has retained this capacity of making any impoverished beggar as much a Muslim as the man who is independent, fearless, and a gentleman: it summons the pauper to worship at the mosque on equal terms at the side of prince and scholar. In the Middle Ages Islam and Christendom confronted each other as two civilisations – Islam, like Russian communism, offering equality without freedom, and Christianity, like American capitalism, torn asunder into rich and poor, offering freedom without social equality.

Whenever an Islamic state was established the ambition of the Islamic divines was the same as that which today fascinates the endeavour of Jewish Orthodoxy in Israel – to have a Western state as well as the Islamic way of life regulated by the laws of the *Shari'a.* Israeli Orthodoxy likewise wants it both ways: a Western state and Jewish Law as interpreted in the Middle Ages. But an informed Western observer of Islam has this to say (*The Times Literary Supplement,* 4th March, 1965): 'As the state formed on a Western model comes increasingly to be the norm in Muslim countries, so the experience of the Muslim believer comes more closely to resemble that of the practising Christian in Western states.' 'Talking of an Islamic system and thinking in terms of the Western system (wrote a Pakistani in 1951) is an incongruity which is visible all around us. The spirit soars to the lofty heights reached in Omar's time, but the eyes are fastened on the spires of Westminster.' What Rosenzweig had to say about a 'Jewish' state Islamic theologians are now saying of an 'Islamic' state. Egypt, which in 1954 adopted a Western constitution, thereby making the United Arab Republic a democratic socialist state, has in consequence of that decision abolished the *Shari'a* courts. Islam is, in Algeria (1963), the 'state religion'; Iraq is a 'democratic socialist state' 'in the spirit of Islam'. How can all this be possible? In fact, of course, it is not possible. The Western state is of Christian origin and it remains a Christian institution. An 'Islamic' Western state is embroiled in the same difficulties which must beset a 'Jewish' Western state. Jews are happy to have achieved the State of Israel; but amid their enthusiastic joy the question has to be asked, 'whither goes the road for the Jew who knows himself to be shaped by the prophets and classical rabbis?'

In Israel, the rabbis of the Sephardic community are totally unaware that their own Sephardic way of life is influenced by Islamic civilisation. No intelligent statement of their difference from either the Ashkenazic community of Israel or from the Israeli political leaders has been forthcoming from the Sephardic rabbis; they merely defend their own vested interest as religious professionals. Something quite different has to be said of the rank and file of the Sephardic community. They form a valuable part of the Israeli people – rooted in the life of their family and, untouched by westernisation, dignified in their practical style of life. This will not, of course, remain so for long. The Israeli army is the great educational instrument of westernisation. Soon the difference between the Sephardic community of Israel that comes straight from the Islamic Middle Ages and the Ashkenazim who come straight from the civilisation of Eastern and Central Europe will have disappeared.

The Islamic situation of the State of Israel was not introduced by the Sephardic Jew, but arises with an inner logic out of a peculiar political predicament. Owing to the electoral system, a socialist party group has to make some concessions to religious Orthodoxy. It is for this most disreputable of reasons that religious Law has been made obligatory for the citizen of Israel. Identification of political law with religious law is Islam: and it is this which now governs the life of the Israeli citizen. A Jewish Orthodoxy, established as 'state religion', is Islam, and something of which Jews cannot, with consistency, approve. A religious state is a caliphate. The fact that in Israel religious law is applied with the support of the state is a step back into the dark ages – into the Islamic Middle Ages. A Jew robbed of his freedom cannot live a Jewish life. We must opt for the West. In the century and a half since Mendelssohn, Jews have proved that they can be both Westerners and Jews.

We see today that Christianity, Islam, and Judaism are disappearing as watertight groups, each separated from the others by their hitherto individual cultures and civilisations. Christian, Muslim, and Jew are all forced into a situation in which they have to assert themselves as three different types. To the Jew, there is nothing new in this situation. The Middle Ages had their two complementary civilisations, the Christian and the Mohammedan. Judaism, with its prophetic roots preserved, never represented a civilisation. If an architect were to reconstruct a model of the Herodian Temple, we would see the kind of building that stood everywhere around the Mediterranean world. The earlier Temple of Solomon was a work of Phoenician architecture. The Hebrew Bible itself has its Canaanite, Egyptian, and Babylonian elements. The Jew, as we have said, is Jew in virtue of his being engaged in *avodah,* worship of God and in work for his livelihood. He is not called upon to erect a 'Jewish' culture. It is only the apocalyptist who will condemn the superstructure over Adam's field as an illusion, and as a quickly fading, sinful Babylon. The so-called superstructure, condemned by the apocalyptist and by the Marxist, is a home for man to live in. It lasts just so long as man can keep out the decay. This he can endeavour to do by his moral

197

actions, by doing justly and by loving mercy. The Jew co-operates with the creators of culture and civilisation. But to speak of a 'Jewish culture' is to be misled by an ideological fallacy. We shall either establish Western civilisation in Israel, or else, if we fail to do so, we shall become involved in Levantine disorder and corruption. By pursuing the phantom of a Jewish culture we cannot preserve our Jewish identity. We must either stand in the midst of Western civilisation as God-worshipping Jews, or we must disappear.

As Western civilisation becomes global civilisation, Christianity and Islam cease to stand apart behind the 'cordon' once provided by their geographical separateness: they now permeate each other. The Christianity of the bourgeois West gains in non-spiritual humaneness; and Islam, adopting the Western state, leaves terrestrial holiness behind and rises to a spiritual status that enables man to become the architect of the superstructure of art and of technical miracles. The Jewish people, divided in the Middle Ages into two groups, one Ashkenazi and the other Sephardi according to their respective habitation in either Christian or Islamic countries, is today losing the complexional differentiation conferred on it by these two different civilisations of the medieval past. After Auschwitz, and after the exodus from the Arab countries, the Jewish people has one cultural prospect only. What is to be mankind's prospect in this new world, in which Christians and Muslims will no longer exist as closed groups separated from each other, and in which the Jew can no longer maintain his distinctive medieval form of life? What is the human situation in an age described by Angelus Silesius, Schelling and Rosenzweig as the Johannine age and today called the post-Constantinian age? It is not the Christian of the Petrine (the Constantinian) Church, with its militant programme of converting non-Western civilisation, who will survive, but rather the Johannine Christian, offering himself, as a Christian person, to the family of man. It is not the Muslim dreaming behind the legalistic walls of his *Shari'a* of an eternity that stands still in human life, who will survive but rather the Muslim as a God-believing humanist, united in equality with his fellow-believer. It is not the Jew integrated into a life of separation by his ritual codes reducing Judaism to a Jewish pietism who will survive; but the Jew who meets God under the same conditions as those under which the Biblical prophet met Him. It is the Jew, the Christian, the Muslim, without the support of their past Jewish, Christian and Islamic cultures, but as three different types of man meeting God in three different ways – these it is who will constitute the future.

INDEX